# CHINA

## Peking and Shandong

TIME-LIFE BOOKS/AMSTERDAM

# COOKERY AROUND THE WORLD

# CHINA Peking and Shandong

**THOMAS GWINNER**

**ZHENHUAN ZHANG**

Food Photography: Michael Brauner

Mongolia

Heilongjiang

Jilin

Xinjiang

Liaoning

Inner Mongolia

Peking

North Korea

Hebei

Tianjin

South Korea

Qinghai

Yellow River

Ningxiaa

Shanxi

Shan-dong

Yellow River

Gansu

Tibet

Henan

Jiangsu

Shaanxi

Japan

Nepal

Bhutan

Shanghai

Sichuan

Hubei

Anhuai

India

Zheijiang

Bangla-desh

Yangtze

Jiangzi

Burma

Hunan

Fujian

Guizhou

Yunnan

Guangxi

Guangdong

Taiwan

Guangzhou (Canton)

Vietnam

Hong Kong

Laos

Thai-land

Hainan

Philippines

0   250   500 km

# CONTENTS

# PEKING AND SHANDONG: RUGGED LAND, RICH CUISINE

Northern China is so different from the south that it is easy to regard the two as entirely different cultures: the "blue" culture of the south and the "yellow" culture of the north. Southern China has a far more moderate climate and geography than the northern half of the country and this has led to rapid growth of both its population and its economy. It contains the country's two largest commercial centres, Shanghai and Canton, and the flat farmlands in the basins of the Yangtze and West rivers produce more than half of China's most vital commodity—rice.

In contrast, northern China is a rugged and unforgiving region that experiences great extremes of weather. Temperatures can dip as low as minus 15-20 degrees centigrade in winter and sandstorms are not unusual. Much of its physical geography is equally bleak, ranging from the craggy mountains of the North Chinese Highlands in the west to the arid Gobi Desert in the north.

In its upper reaches the Yellow River—the main waterway of northern China—flows through a landscape of barren steppes and eroded gullies. Growing anything on the land here is hard, as centuries of erosion have washed the topsoil off the hills. Where the soil has been deposited downstream, however, the potential for agriculture is much better. The great plain around the mouth of the river, with Peking (Beijing) to the northeast, accounts for 20 per cent of the nation's farmland and is easily the most densely populated area in northern China.

Whilst the Yellow River has provided the Shandong area with fertile farmland, it has also brought its share of misery to the local inhabitants. In China's long history the river has breached its banks more than 1,500 times, drowning an estimated 10 million Chinese. Only in recent years has the pattern of drought and flood been contained through river regulation and the construction of huge dams.

The bleak environment and harsh struggle against the elements has naturally influenced the character of the people of northern China. To outsiders they appear down-to-earth, conservative and dependable, with neither the great adaptability of the Cantonese nor the quick wit of the people of Shanghai. It is perhaps due to the inhospitality of the climate and the effect it has on their way of life, that food has always been one of the greatest sources of pleasure to the northern Chinese. Their love of good food is reflected in the delightfully poetic names that they have given to even the plainest of dishes.

Down through the ages many delicious specialities have been created in northern China, and to include the culinary styles of all its regions would have taken a series of books. We have therefore devoted this volume mainly to the cuisine of the two most famous areas—Peking and Shandong. Many of their most popular dishes have been adopted in the other northern provinces, where they complement the lesser-known regional cuisine.

Northern China has long been regarded as the cradle of Chinese civilization and the heart of the Middle Kingdom, so it is hardly surprising that so many of China's most exquisite dishes originated in this part of the country. In the recipe sections you will find the pick of them, lavishly illustrated with easy-to-follow instructions. Also included is information about important local produce used in northern Chinese cookery and a glossary at the end of the book explains ingredients, cooking methods and utensils. Finally, the menu suggestions will help you select suitable dishes to prepare for your own authentic northern Chinese meals.

# HEART OF THE MIDDLE KINGDOM

**P**eking and the surrounding province of Shandong have long dominated northeastern China, both politically and socially. Not surprisingly, this influence has extended into the sphere of cooking as well. Whilst this book concentrates mainly on the capital, it also focuses on those provinces where the culinary styles of Peking and Shandong have mixed with local methods and recipes to produce dishes which contain the best of both.

Hebei—the area around Peking—together with Shandong to the southeast and Henan to the south make up the great plain of north China. This agricultural basin provides those same provinces—and the neighbouring mountainous regions of Shanxi and Shaanxi—with the food the huge population needs to survive. The climate of northern China is too harsh to cultivate rice, the traditional Chinese staple. Instead, for thousands of years, winter wheat has been grown in the broad terraces which line the Yellow River basin and the valleys of the vast loess region further inland.

The northern Chinese plain is one of the country's most important agricultural areas. It produces maize, millet, barley and other cereals, as well as a multitude of vegetables including Chinese cabbage, leeks, garlic and peppers. In addition to Peking, the country's capital, the plain also encompasses Tianjin, a major port and industrial and administrative centre.

Peking's famous style of cookery has developed from many different sources. The imperial court attracted people from all over the country, and because of Peking's proximity to the great steppes, the city's cuisine also owes much to the influence of the nomadic tribes. The province of Shandong not only has a long coast bordering the Yellow Sea, but also has extensive mountain regions. As a result, cooks have always been able to choose between cooking fish and seafood specialities or aromatic mushroom and game dishes. Although it has much in common with the cuisine of the capital, Shandong cooking has the more ancient tradition of the two. It has managed to retain its own distinct style, which is more robust and strongly flavoured. Such was its reputation that many Ming emperors summoned the best cooks from Shandong to their courts.

When the last emperor, Pu Yi, was overthrown in 1911, the imperial chefs suddenly found themselves without an employer. Of those that stayed in Peking, a few decided to open restaurants recreating the famous cuisine of the imperial court. The best-known of these, Fangshan, is now one of the most exclusive restaurants in all of China.

*The Peking Opera sets the style for opera in the rest of China. The costumes and make-up are extraordinarily elaborate and the slightest change in movement or tone can be significant.*

## The Capital: Peking

Peking—or Beijing as the name of the city is written in pinyin characters—has had a long and convoluted history. Its name and its status changed constantly from its foundation around 3,000 years ago, when it was known as Ji, until 1421 when it became China's capital under the Ming dynasty.

From 400 BC until 1215 AD, when the city was destroyed by the Mongols, Ji was variously called Yanjing (capital of the Yan empire), Youzhou, Nanjing (southern capital) and Zhongdu (middle capital). Kublai Khan chose the city as his seat of government and had it reconstructed at the end of the 13th century, calling it Dadu (great capital).

At first the Ming dynasty (1368-1644) chose Nanking as their capital and Dadu became Beiping (northern peace). Fifty-three years later, however, Emperor Yong Le reversed this decision and Beiping became the seat of government once more, finally changing its name to Peking (northern capital). By moving the centre of power northwards to the city on the edge of the steppes, and then building the Great Wall, the Emperor hoped to be in a better position to defend his realm against the constant threat from the Mongol tribes of the north.

Peking's famous "Forbidden City" was built around this time. Although it sounds mysterious, this "city" was actually the imperial palace—a whole complex of buildings, towers and halls to which only the imperial family, prominent dignitaries and members of the imperial household were allowed access. For those who dared to breach the high red ramparts of the palace without proper authority, the penalty was instant death. It was only after the 1911 revolution that a network of streets was constructed around the Forbidden City, and the "City within the city" was integrated into Peking life.

After World War II, Peking underwent dramatic changes. With the help of the Soviet Union, the Communist rulers attempted to transform imperial Peking into the model of a socialist metropolis. Ancient buildings were pulled down to make way for factories, huge apartment blocks and neo-classical showcase buildings. Fortunately the Imperial Palace, the Temple of Heaven, the Summer Palace and its adjacent Bethai Park were spared from the general orgy of destruction. Among the socially inspiring edifices built during this period are the Great Hall of the People and the Museum of the Chinese Revolution in Tianenmen Square, or the "Square of Heavenly Peace".

Right in the heart of the city, Tianenmen Square bursts with life by both day and night. On warm summer evenings people escape from their small, stuffy flats and pass the time chatting or playing cards. The older sections of the city are made up mostly of small warren-like courtyards

surrounded by small one-storey flats. From the street, the only way into these yards is to squeeze through a narrow entrance between the houses. Trees planted in the centre of the courtyards provide shade and an illusion of calm. Flowers and vegetables are grown in the yards and it is not uncommon to find chickens and ducks flapping around.

To house the ever-growing population, the Communist government initiated a building programme that culminated with the erection of large, soulless blocks of flats on the outskirts of the city. Most residents, however, are quite happy to exchange their old inner-city homes for one of these modern apartments. Despite what the tourists may think, they find nothing at all "romantic" about living without water, electricity or even sanitation.

The best way to explore Peking is to hire a bicycle and join the incredible chaotic throng of cyclists, cars, lorries, taxis and buses. Although it may look dangerous, a bike is still the safest and simplest way to reach sights such as the Gate of Supreme Harmony and Mao's mausoleum. The Summer Palace, about 15 kilometres north of Peking, is well worth a visit, though those with less sturdy legs may prefer to take a taxi. Finding something to keep you going while you are out and about is not usually a problem. Street stalls and markets sell an amazing array of foods that are often too tempting to resist. Try not to feel too guilty if you succumb—just pedal a bit harder afterwards!

*The Hall of Supreme Harmony, where the emperor once granted audiences, stands in the southern quarter of the Forbidden City.*

*In Peking, as in the rest of China, the bicycle continues to be the main form of transport.*

## The Lowland Plain of Northern China

The region on the lower reaches of the Huang He, or Yellow River, encompasses the three provinces of Hebei, Henan and Shandong. Archaeological finds have confirmed that this lowland plain of northern China and the neighbouring loess mountain country to the west saw the first beginnings of Chinese civilization. The earliest recorded state, the Yin or Shang empire, rose up here around the middle of the second millennium BC.

### Hebei Province

Tianjin, a seaport vital to the region's economy, and Peking lie within the borders of Hebei, although both cities are actually distinct provinces in their own right. Among the finest monuments of the region is the former imperial residence on the northern outskirts of the city of Chengde, about 250 kilometres northeast of Peking. Formerly a sleepy provincial town, Chengde was transformed when Emperor Kan XI commissioned the construction of a splendid summer palace there. It was built between 1703 and 1711 in a picturesque setting of gnarled old pine trees. Today's visitors can still admire the throne room, the proclamation hall and the emperor's apartments.

Chengde itself is now a typical northern Chinese industrial centre, complete with factories and mines. The streets come to life very early in the morning, as they do all over China. In the market traders selling fresh produce, especially Chinese cabbages stacked in great towering piles, loudly ply their wares.

About 300 kilometres east of Peking, not far from the Great Wall, is the seaside town of Beidaihe, a popular holiday resort. Work on a wall here to repel the Mongol hordes dates back to the middle of the first century BC. Over the centuries it was repeatedly extended, pulled down, rebuilt and extended again. The best-preserved section of the wall is near Ba da ling, about 85 km northeast of Peking. By early morning, the wall is thronged with tourists and souvenir sellers, so the best time to visit is just after dawn.

## Henan Province

On the fertile plain south of the Yellow River stands Kaifeng, one of the most ancient imperial cities in China. The city has retained much of its traditional character, with ornate wooden facades and narrow streets where markets, shops and stalls still operate much as they did hundreds of years ago.

An unmissable sight, set amidst the Songshan mountain chain, is the Shaolin Monastery, a building that has featured in numerous films. Here, the founding fathers of Chan Buddhism (better known by the Japanese spelling, Zen) developed a method of unarmed combat so that the monks living alone in the mountains could protect themselves against bandits. Their system of defensive stances and movements later became known as Kung Fu or Shaolin boxing.

## Shandong Province

Shandong is renowned not only for its fertile and charming landscape but also as the birthplace of Confucius, China's great teacher and philosopher, who lived from 551 to 479 BC. Like many great thinkers, during his lifetime Confucius was never accorded true recognition. It was only under the Han dynasty some 300 years after his death that his teachings were elevated to official doctrine. The huge and opulent Temple of Confucius in the town of Qufu was built in his honour between the 16th and 18th centuries.

According to the teachings of Confucius, a person should exercise self-control and strive for virtue, compassion and honesty. In this way they will achieve nobility, irrespective of their social status. He viewed society as a hierachical system, however, which could be broken down into what he termed the "five relationships". According to this concept a servant is subordinate to his master, a wife to her husband, a younger brother to his older brother, a younger friend to an older friend and children to their parents.

With its strong sense of morality, and its emphasis on conservative values and a strict framework of relationships, Confucianism was extremely popular with successive imperial dynasties. These same teachings, though, meant that it was rejected out of hand by Mao Zedong and his egalitarian Communist party. But two thousand years of belief could not be destroyed in less than half a century, even by Mao. Despite fierce official disapproval, Confucianism never disappeared completely and, since the end of the Cultural Revolution, it has been steadily rising in popularity once again.

*The beach at Beidaihe, a favourite holiday and health resort on the Yellow Sea coast.*

*The Puning Temple near Chengde was built in 1755. Lamaistic Buddhist monks still live and worship here.*

## The Land of the
## Loess Mountains

### Shaanxi Province

Xi'an, the capital of Shaanxi province, is another of China's ancient imperial cities. It was the capital of China under the Tang Dynasty (618-906 AD), when it was called Chang'an, meaning long-lasting peace. For a time it was the largest metropolis in the world. It was here that merchants following the Silk Road, the legendary caravan route through Asia, arrived to trade western gold, silver and wool for eastern silk.

Many different religions and their buildings of worship have withstood the changing patterns of Chinese history. There are an estimated 30,000 Muslims, or *Hui*, living in Xi'an, the men instantly recognizable by their beards and white caps. Most reside in the area immediately around the great mosque, a huge building that dates back to the Ming period of the middle ages. With the relaxation of Communist restrictions on religion, people are now also free to worship at the Buddhist, Lamaist and Taoist temples. This diverse mix of beliefs illustrates the cosmopolitan character of old Xi'an.

The palace of Emperor Qin Shi Huangdi, who reigned between 221 and 210 BC, is believed to have stood to the northwest of the city, on the north bank of the River Wei. Although the actual building has not survived, in 1974 excavations of the Emperor's tomb uncovered the now famous Terracotta Army, a collection of over 7,000 warriors created to protect the Emperor in the afterlife.

The loess plateau covers the northern half of Shaanxi Province. This is an area of high plains where, over the centuries, erosion has created bizarre valleys of all shapes and sizes. Set amidst this landscape, some 270 kilometres north of Xi'an, is Yan'an, a small town that has become synonymous with the Communist movement. In 1934, 100,000 people broke through the encircling forces of Chiang Kai-shek's Kuomintang army and began a retreat that became known as the Long March. They fought a constant battle against the Kuomintang, bandits and the elements until, over a year later, Mao and just 8,000 survivors finally found safety at Yan'an.

With such a sudden influx of people, housing space was at a premium. Many of the prominent party and military leaders were forced to make their homes in caves, much as local peasant families had done for centuries—and indeed still do today. Like many other northern Chinese homes, they are equipped with the traditional *kang*, a bed made from clay bricks, heated from inside like an oven to combat the cold.

*Buddhist monks take care of the many temples dotted around the slopes of Wutaishan mountain.*

## Shanxi Province

Two of China's most important Buddhist monuments, the Yungang Grottos and the sacred mountain Wutaishan, can be found in the province of Shanxi.

Buddhism is the newcomer of China's three main religions. First appearing around the first century AD, it had spread along the Silk Road from India and quickly rose to become as popular as Taoism and Confucianism. The Yungang Grottos were carved into the sandstone on the southern slopes of the Wuzhou mountain chain between 453 and 495 AD. Some 15,000 statues and reliefs have been preserved in more than 53 grottos spread over a kilometre of mountainside. At one time there are believed to have been double that number but the grottos have suffered from the weather. Even so, those that remain are an astonishing sight.

The imposing Wutaishan mountain in the east of Shanxi province is 200 kilometres away from the provincial capital, Taiyuan. The summit of Wutaishan is dotted with 58 strikingly beautiful temples, some of which have been carefully restored in the last few decades. The mountain has long been a place of Buddhist pilgrimage, reaching a peak of popularity under the Tang dynasty (618-906 AD), when people would journey from as far afield as Japan, Nepal and Indonesia.

Not only does Shanxi contain one of the four mountains holy to Buddhists but it also holds within its borders Mount Hengshan, one of the five mythical Chinese mountains. At one time emperors made sacrifices to the gods of heaven on its slopes. Now it is best known for the hanging monastery, Xunakong Si, which clings precariously to the cliff face, anchored by wooden beams driven into clefts in the rock. Built in the sixth century AD, the monastery houses extensive displays of sculptures and ancient pottery.

*The largest of the images of Buddha in the Yungang Grottoes is 17 metres high, the smallest a mere 2 cm.*

*Wrapped up in their thick clothing, these two children are well protected against the cold of the northern Chinese winter.*

*Striking a balance between the five flavours—sweet, sour, bitter, pungent and salty—is equally important to a chef, whether preparing a grand feast in a restaurant or cooking a simple meal at home.*

## Cookery and a Philosophy of Life

Since primeval times, good food has always been accorded the highest importance in the Middle Kingdom. Food has never been overabundant in any part of the country—except, of course, at the imperial court. For centuries the harvest has been threatened alternately with droughts and floods and, despite advances in agriculture and technology, the danger is still there today. In northern China they have striven—not always successfully—to protect themselves and their crops from the ravages of the Yellow River, knowing that to fail could mean misery and starvation.

In the course of time, food and its preparation developed into something more complex than simple sustenance: it became an expression of social and philosophical principles. The teachings of men such as Confucius and Mencius have been refined over the centuries into a widely accepted philosophy. Central to this is the recognition of the close relationship between man and the environment. As it says in an ancient Chinese cookery book: "Eating and drinking serve to support life. Frivolity and fickleness in these matters may damage a person... if one takes care over food and drink, but only attaches importance to pleasant flavours, then one will not find the balance between the benefits and harm caused by food."

Chinese cookery requires relatively few refined ingredients. It is possible to conjure up exquisite meals from the simplest components. The aim is for each individual dish to be a harmonious mix of elements, which in turn should be compatible with the rest of the menu. This harmony is achieved through skilful blending and the observation of certain simple rules. The principle of yin and yang—symbolized by a circle divided into two interlocking shapes, one black and one white—applies when a dish is composed of just two elements. Originally, yin meant the shadowy side of a mountain; it stands for darkness, passivity and femininity. Yang meant the sunny slopes of the mountain, and signifies light, activity and masculinity. The Chinese believe that an ingredient is either one or the other and if an effective balance is not achieved then the body will suffer.

Yi Yin, who lived around the 16th century BC, is credited as being the first Chinese gastronome. He held that to obtain perfection foods should not only be divided into yin and yang, but that a meal should also contain each of the five elements—earth, wood, metal, fire and water—which correspond to the five flavours: sweet, sour, bitter, pungent and salty. In addition, foods are categorised as cold, cool, warm or hot. This refers less to the temperature foods are served at, than to the feeling they create after being eaten. In winter it is customary to serve more "hot" foods such as grilled or fried spiced meat, while summer dishes of salads, fruit and vegetables are light and refreshing. Regardless of the time of year, however, a well-balanced yin-yang menu should include all five flavours and all four temperature radiations.

One Chinese author writing in the early 14th century summed up the Chinese philosophy of food as follows: "The best way to protect and nourish the body is to practise restraint... if one exercises care and moderation in eating and drinking, if one does not wake or sleep without reason, if, by means of the five flavours, one creates harmony between the five organs (liver, heart, spleen, lungs and kidneys), then blood and energy will be supplied in good measure, the spirit will be healthy and happy, and the mind and thoughts will be balanced and firm..."

*Although most Chinese still buy their produce fresh from the market, supermarkets stocking pre-packed goods, like this one in Peking, are becoming increasingly popular in the larger cities.*

## From the Kitchens of Shandong to the Imperial Palace

Although internationally the cuisine of Shandong is not so well known as that of Peking, the Shandong style of cooking is just as varied and enjoyable. Typically, dishes are highly seasoned with plenty of garlic, but they can also often be more subtly flavoured with coriander, ginger or spring onion.

Rice is hardly used at all. Instead cereal crops such as wheat, sorghum (a kind of millet), maize and sweet potatoes are included to give dishes more substance. Vegetables like Chinese cabbage, aubergines and a variety of turnips are widely popular and the local garlic is thought to be the best in all of China. Since the province is blessed with both a long sea coast and an extensive mountain range, local cooks are able to choose between fish, seafood and sharks' fins, as well as game and exotic mushrooms.

Shandong cuisine has long had an enviable reputation. Ming emperors from the 14th to the 17th centuries insisted on having Shandong cooks in charge of the courtly kitchens. Indeed, it would probably be more accurate if the now world-famous Peking duck was called Shandong duck instead.

Throughout history, the culinary arts have played an important role in Chinese culture and society, flourishing more in political and economic centres than in other parts of the country. Peking, the capital since 1421, has benefited more than most from a concentration of expertise. Peking cuisine has often been thought to have evolved from the creations of the cooks at the imperial palace. Though no-one could afford the extravagance of the court, many tried to emulate it as closely as they could. In time cookery became an accurate indicator of social status—the higher your place in society, the closer the quality of your kitchen to the emperor's. Gradually, distinct styles developed.

Kong, or Confucian, cookery was originally created by the famous family of the same name. In its artistic presentation and preparation it was similar to that practised in the palace kitchens, the main distinction being that less expensive ingredients were used. With certain limitations, the same could be said of the cuisine of China's powerful public servants, the Mandarins, of whom the Tan family in Peking were probably the most famous.

Further down the social scale would have been numerous other grades of northern Chinese cookery, including the acclaimed vegetarian cooking of some of the religious temples and a variety of peasant styles. Of course there were no strict boundaries between the various styles, and it was inevitable that, over

*Whilst lamb and beef are popular winter fare all over China, the northern Chinese—apart from the Muslim community—are particularly partial to pork.*

*Chinese cabbage is an important source of vitamins during the winter.*

time, the differences became less pronounced as each variation adopted ideas from the others.

In order to excite the emperor with ever more exotic delights, palace cooks would conjure up extraordinary dishes containing ingredients such as swallows' nests and bears' paws. The desire to sample such dishes may even have led some to aspire to the imperial throne. According to legend, Yi Yin was describing the finest delicacies to King Tang, who asked if Yi Yin could prepare them for him. Yi Yin replied: "Your kingdom is small. It is not large enough for you to have them brought to your home and prepared for you there. Only if you became the Son of Heaven [the emperor] could they be made for you."

Palace cooks also went to great lengths to impress their emperor with the speed with which they could prepare meals or obtain different foods. One Tang emperor, Ming Huang, and his favourite concubine, Yang Guife, were particularly fond of litchis,

which unfortunately only grew in southern China. To cater for their tastes a non-stop pony express was established whose sole purpose was to transport the fruit to the palace as soon as it had been picked. A more recent example of extravagance comes from the last days of the Qing dynasty, when large numbers of servants were kept busy stuffing bean sprouts for the Empress Dowager Ci Xi. Among her other favourites was "pearl tofu"—a simple but expensive dish consisting of pearls and tofu, continuously boiled together for 49 days.

As a rule, however, the emperor had little influence over his menu. The palace cooks presented him with hundreds of different dishes, making it impossible to taste them all. Eunuchs took careful note of what he ate and how much. At the least sign of indisposition the court dieticians concocted a remedy which the emperor was obliged to swallow. It was not always fun to be the Son of Heaven!

*The palace lions in the Forbidden City were once symbols of the power of the emperor.*

## "White Jade Set in Gold": The Naming of Chinese Dishes

Most Chinese dishes are named after specific ingredients, the method of preparation, a special seasoning or the place where they were first created. Others owe their names to their inventor or to a famous person, to which there is usually a story attached.

In northern China, as in the rest of the country, creating poetic titles for dishes is a favourite pastime. Thus the impressive-sounding "Phoenix" in a title is probably a cover for the humble chicken, while "silver shoots" refers to nothing more exotic than mung bean sprouts. This linguistic ennoblement can at times be amusing and at others impressive, but it can also lead to disappointment, as illustrated in the following three stories.

In ancient China there lived a district administrator who had a reputation as

a great gourmet. However, he set as much store by the elaborate and romantic names for the dishes prepared in his kitchen as in the food itself. Over the years he sacked many excellent cooks because they had no talent for inventing fancy titles.

One morning, news of this gourmet reached the ears of a none-too-gifted cook who had a well-developed sense of humour. He immediately presented himself at the administrator's house and applied for a job. Such were the boasts of the man's poetic flair that the administrator appointed him straight away. For lunch, the new cook announced that he would prepare two dishes: "Dark clouds cover the sun" and "The green dragon crosses the sea". His employer was so delighted he could hardly contain his excitement. He sat down at the table much earlier than usual, eagerly anticipating his midday meal.

Eventually, the new cook emerged from the kitchen. He set before the administrator an empty yellow bowl and a pair of chopsticks, on top of which he placed a pancake, blackened and burnt to a crisp. "Dark clouds cover the sun," he proclaimed, "please help yourself," and before his employer could utter a word, he disappeared back to the kitchen to prepare the second course. After a while he returned, and served a bowl of water in which floated a solitary green piece of spring onion. "The green dragon crosses the sea", the administrator muttered under his breath.

The second story tells of a time when the Qing Emperor Qian Long (1711-1799) was travelling through the south of China. The provisions for the

imperial party suddenly ran out and there was no alternative but to call at a nearby farmhouse and order the farmer to prepare a meal for the Emperor. All the poor man had to hand was tofu and some green spinach with red roots. He was uneasy about setting such simple fare before his honoured guest, but he had no choice. First he deep-fried the tofu, then tossed it with the spinach leaves and roots in hot oil. Hunger adds its own flavour, however, and to the farmer's relief, the Emperor thoroughly enjoyed the modest meal. When he asked what it was called the farmer was prepared: "White jade set in gold, green parrot with a red beak."

The third tale is a modern one. A Western businessman was entertaining some Chinese clients in a famous restaurant. He spoke perfect Chinese and was well versed in local etiquette, and he played his role as host with great expertise, selecting and ordering food for the entire table. The guests glanced down at their menus, studying the delightful but unfamiliar names of the dishes, and eagerly anticipating the meal ahead.

Afterwards the guests warmly congratulated their host on his excellent choice of dishes, which had combined to create a perfect meal. They were doubly impressed because, they admitted, they had not known what lay behind such exotic titles as "golden needles with strips of silver" and would have had to ask the waiter to help them order. The Western businessman basked in their praise for a while, but after a few drinks could not resist revealing his secret. The waiter had not realized that he could read Chinese and so handed him a bilingual menu. This showed not only the lyrical Chinese names but also listed, in plain English, clear descriptions of what was in each dish.

*Even in the most highly populated country on earth there are still places where one can enjoy complete tranquillity, such as the inner courtyard of the Tanzhe Temple, near Peking.*

*Breakfast for many Chinese consists of steamed noodles from a roadside stall.*

*A woman selling incense sticks for worshippers to burn in the nearby Buddhist temple.*

## The Everyday and the Festive

Traditionally, there are few single-person households in China and, as a rule, both husband and wife go out to work. Shopping, therefore, has to be done either early in the morning or on the way home in the evening. In Chinese society this is almost always the woman's responsibility. Despite the Communists' introduction of the "marriage law of the People's Republic of China", which embraced equal rights for women in 1950s, discrimination is still very much the woman's lot: it will take more than a couple of generations to break the male domination that has persisted for thousands of years. Women in China still have the worst-paid jobs and are seldom found in positions of power in either the Party, in commerce or in industry.

Being part of a family is incredibly important to the Chinese. Grand-parents, parents and children see themselves as forming a single unit and will often either share the same house or at least live very close to each other. This is a great help for many working mothers as they can rely on the grandparents to look after the children, or more usually child, during the day.

The state's policy of encouraging one child per family by taxing parents with two or more has had enormous social impact. The traditional extended family of aunts, uncles and cousins will soon be a thing of the past. A whole generation are growing up as only children, inevitably having the love of both parents and grandparents lavished upon them. Nevertheless, in the countryside, where people have been slower to realize the penalties of having more than one child, there are still traditionally large households where three or even four generations live together under one roof.

Right from birth, every Chinese belongs to a *danwei*, or work unit, which in many ways is similar to an extended family. Although the *danwei*'s main task is to ensure employment for both husband and wife, and even for their children when the time comes, its influence extends far beyond the workplace. For instance, it takes care of housing, gives permission to marry (to women at the age of 20 and men at 22) and is responsible for health care. As change spreads through the Chinese economy, however, these organizations are beginning to disappear. Today, many young people are sacrificing the security of the *danwei* to take their chances with the emerging new capitalist system.

When the morning's shopping is done, many Chinese breakfast at a stall on the way to work. This meal may consist of steamed wheat noodles, thin rice broth with chunks of vegetables, or hot soya milk. Lunch is eaten in the works canteen or at home and is usually a selection of several cold and hot dishes accompanied by noodles.

Unlike the individual portions which Europeans are used to, food is placed in large bowls in the centre of the table and everyone helps themselves with chopsticks or small porcelain spoons. On festive occasions the host will serve the guests of honour, seated to his left and right, with separate portions on individual plates using special chopsticks. If you are invited to a meal in a Chinese home, remember never to leave a plate, bowl or glass totally empty. Your host would take this to mean that there was not enough to eat or drink and that you are still hungry.

Major events like family gatherings or birthdays are always celebrated with something special to eat. Neither time,

money nor imagination are spared in the effort to produce a suitably impressive array of dishes. This is especially true during the Spring Festival, the most important of all Chinese celebrations, which falls, according to the lunar calendar, between late January and early February. Preparations for the feast begin at least a week in advance and women can be seen heading home from the market with baskets laden with meat, fish and vegetables.

On the actual Spring Festival day, the cooking is relatively quick, but each of the dishes must be freshly prepared in turn and all the ingredients have to be washed, trimmed, chopped or shredded. Unfortunately this means that the cook can only join the family for soup at the end of the meal: he—or most probably she—spends the rest of the meal hidden away in the kitchen. A fish dish is invariably served at the festival and some is always left uneaten to ensure a surplus of food in the coming year. Similarly, at a birthday celebration the menu must include long noodles, as these symbolize long life.

*Government family planning policy means there are now a large number of only children in China. Bringing them up to have a sense of community presents Chinese society with an enormous challenge.*

*Even today, northern Chinese farmers separate the grain from the chaff by hand.*

## Drinks and Drinking

The Chinese have a word, *jiu*, which encompasses all of the many and varied alcoholic drinks that can be found in the Middle Kingdom. In translations of old Chinese poems—some of which were undoubtedly composed under the influence of alcohol—*jiu* is almost always written as "wine". This is

somewhat misleading, as wine, or at least wine pressed from grapes, was practically unheard of in ancient China. The nearest thing to it was a sweet form of grape wine which could be found in oases in the extreme northwest of the country.

Only since the 1980s, when joint ventures were set up with French and Italian wine growers, have grapes been cultivated in any quantity. Dry and medium-dry white, rosé and red wines are all now produced in the northeastern provinces of Hebei and Shandong. Most Chinese are still not quite accustomed to the taste of the dryer white wines or the more bitter reds, and so sweet, fruity varieties are the most popular.

Wine still has a long way to go to match the popularity of beer, even though this is another relative newcomer. The first brewery, Tsingtao, was established in Shandong early this century by a German company. Since then, beer consumption has risen incredibly. According to statistics, in 1993 over twelve thousand million litres of the beverage were produced, making China second only to the USA as the world's largest brewer of beer. Each province has its own brands and breweries, which often have trouble keeping up with the massive demand, especially in summer. China's most famous beer is still "Tsingtao", named after the original brewery; locally, Peking's best-known brands are "Beijing" and "Yanjing"—an old name for the city.

The German influence on Chinese beer-making has somehow survived the multitude of changes that China has undergone during the last century. In recent years there has been increased cooperation between German and Chinese companies. There is now even a Chinese school for master brewers at Wuhan, in Hubei province.

Despite beer's phenomenal success the favourite drinks in China are still the same as they were 2,000 years ago: rice wine and spirits. Rice wine—known as *huang jiu* or *Shaoxing jiu*, after the famous winery at Shaoxing in the province of Zhejiang—is China's traditional alcoholic beverage. It is usually consumed at room temperature, but many people like to drink it warm in winter.

Spirits are mostly distilled from sorghum, a type of millet, to which other cereals are then added. Their average alcoholic content is between 53 and 56 per cent. In northern China, especially in the northeastern provinces, consumption of spirits is high, particularly during the long, cold winter months when they are said to warm up both the body and the soul.

Drinking in Chinese society, as in many other cultures, is usually a social activity; indeed, in the countryside everyone shares the same large bowl. City-dwellers prefer to drink their rice wine or spirit from small porcelain cups or glasses. The widely-used expression for "cheers"—*ganbei*—literally means "drink the cup dry", as it is customary to drain the contents in one gulp.

Drinking games are popular in China. For one of these, players need a good knowledge of poetry: someone quotes a line of a poem, then the next person must recite the following line. If they cannot, the "punishment" is a glassful of spirit. In the north and throughout

China, the most popular drinking game is the finger game. On a specific command two opponents stretch out a number of fingers, between none and five, keeping their hands hidden from their opponent. At the top of their voices, often in short impromptu verse, they then try to guess the total number of fingers being held out. If one guesses correctly, his opponent has to drink a glassful straight down; if no-one wins then the game is repeated.

Small spicy snacks are always served when drinking in company. The fieriness of the seasoning is said to complement the drinks on the one hand and, on the other, to prevent the drinkers from succumbing too quickly to the effects of the alcohol.

Finally, there is a well-known Chinese proverb about meeting someone for a drink: "If you meet a dear friend, a thousand cups are too few—if two people talk at cross purposes, half a cup is too much."

*Although tea is not actually grown in the north it is still a popular drink, especially in winter when it is the most common alternative to alcohol.*

# COLD STARTERS

I n China any festive meal begins with a choice of cold starters. Throughout the land, whether at a restaurant or entertaining at home, it is customary to serve the guests with a selection of beautifully presented cold appetizers as soon as they sit down at the table.

For the Chinese, a successful dish must have three basic characteristics: a pleasing appearance (*'se*), a pleasant smell (*xiang*), and a good flavour (*wei*). With starters, there is particular emphasis on *'se*. Using the most modest ingredients, expert cooks can fashion appetizers into wonderful shapes, such as a dragon, a phoenix or even a landscape. Fortunately, these snacks taste just as delicious when prepared with less dexterity.

Cold starters are intended simply to whet the appetite, so they are quite often strong and piquant in flavour, and served in small quantities. In China they always accompany the glass of spirit or rice wine that men still like to drink in a tavern when they finish work. The pungent or spicy flavour of the appetizers complements the drink, while at the same time the food lines the stomach, preventing the alcohol from rushing to the head.

# Pork with garlic

*Simple • Summer dish*    **Suan ni bai rou**    *Serves 2*

**200 g boned belly of pork, with rind (about 3 cm thick)**
**1 thin slice fresh ginger root**
**1 tsp rice wine**
**salt**
**3 garlic cloves**
**2 tsp light soy sauce**
**1 tsp sesame oil**

**Preparation time: 45 minutes**

**1,800 kJ/430 calories per portion**

**1** Wash the pork. Place it in a fireproof casserole or saucepan and add ½ litre water. Bring to the boil over medium heat. Add the ginger, rice wine and a little salt. Cover and simmer over low heat for about 30 minutes.

**2** Remove the cooked meat from the saucepan and leave it to cool for about 5 minutes, then cut the meat across the grain into slices about 5 cm long and 2 mm thick. Arrange the slices on a serving plate.

**3** Peel and finely chop the garlic. Mix it with the soy sauce and sesame oil and pour the mixture over the sliced meat.

**Note:** If you find belly of pork too fatty, you can use a leaner cut. The garlic can be crushed in a garlic press, if preferred, but it gives the dish a stronger flavour when chopped. This dish looks very attractive if it is garnished with decorative sweet pepper shapes, such as Chinese characters, but they do take patience and dexterity. It is simpler if you use a special cutter.

# Beef with five spices

*Easy • Autumn dish* **Wu xiang jiang rou** *Serves 4*

**500 g tender beef (for example, fillet), about 4 cm thick**
**1 spring onion**
**1 walnut-sized piece fresh ginger root**
**10 Sichuan peppercorns**
**3 pieces star anise**
**1 cinnamon stick • 2 cloves**
**2 tsp fennel seeds • 1 tbsp rice wine**
**2 tbsp dark soy sauce • salt**
**cucumber and carrot slices, and leek leaves, to garnish (optional)**

**Preparation time: 25 minutes (plus 45 minutes' cooking time)**

**670 kJ/160 calories per portion**

**1** Wash the meat. Place it in a fireproof casserole or saucepan and add enough water to cover the meat and bring to the boil. Meanwhile, trim and wash the spring onion, peel the ginger, and split the cinnamon stick in half lengthwise. Place the Sichuan peppercorns, star anise, cinnamon stick, cloves and the fennel seeds in a small muslin bag, and tie securely.

**2** When the water comes to the boil, add the spring onion, ginger, spice bag, rice wine, soy sauce and a little salt. Cover the pan and simmer over low heat for about 45 minutes. Remove the meat from the stock and leave to cool.

**3** Boil the stock over high heat, stirring constantly, until it is reduced by half. Cut the meat into slices about 7 cm long and 5 mm thick.

**4** Arrange the meat slices on a long serving dish and pour 2 to 3 tbsp stock over them. Serve garnished with slices of cucumber and carrot, and leek, cut into leaf shapes, if liked.

**Variation:** Instead of the bag of spices. use Chinese five-spice powder, which is a mixture of anise pepper, fennel seed, cassia, star anise and cloves. Sprinkle 1 tbsp of powder into the boiling water.

# Prawns with cabbage

*Easy • Shandong*

**Xia ban bai cai xin**

*Serves 3 to 4*

**250 g unpeeled raw prawns**
**1 spring onion**
**1 thin slice fresh ginger root**
**5 Sichuan peppercorns**
**salt**
**1 tbsp rice wine**
**250 g young Chinese cabbage leaves**
**rind of 2 unwaxed mandarin oranges (about 10 g)**
**75 g sugar**
**2 tbsp white rice vinegar**

*Preparation time: 40 minutes*

*620 kJ/150 calories per portion (if serving 4)*

**1** Wash the prawns, cut off the feelers, but leave the heads on. Bring a large saucepan of water to the boil, add the prawns and cook in the briskly boiling water for about 1 minute. Pour away the water. Trim and wash the spring onion and cut into pieces about 10 cm long. Peel the ginger.

**2** Bring 35 cl water to the boil in a saucepan, then add the prawns, spring onion, ginger and Sichuan peppercorns. Season with salt and rice wine. When the water comes to the boil, cook the prawns over medium heat for about 3 minutes. Remove from the heat, cover and leave to stand for 10 minutes.

**3** Remove the cooked prawns from the pan, drain and arrange on a serving plate. Discard the spring onion pieces.

**4** Wash the Chinese cabbage and pat dry. Cut the leaves lengthwise into very thin shreds, then crosswise to make the shreds about 6 cm long.

**5** Wash the mandarin rind, pat dry and shred very finely. Reserve a little of the rind. Place the remaining rind in a bowl with the shredded cabbage, sugar and rice vinegar, and mix thoroughly, then arrange the cabbage around the edge of the serving plate. Sprinkle the rest of the rind over the prawns and serve.

# Chicken with mustard

*Easy • Summer dish*

**Jie mo ji si**

*Serves 4*

**200 g skinned, boneless chicken breast**
**1 tsp rice wine**
**salt**
**200 g bean sprouts**
**1 carrot for garnish (optional)**

**For the sauce:**
**1 tbsp medium-hot mustard**
**1 tsp light soy sauce**
**1 tsp white rice vinegar**
**1 tbsp sesame oil**

*Preparation time: 40 minutes*

*380 kJ/90 calories per portion*

**1** Place the chicken breast in a small saucepan with about ½ litre water and bring to the boil over medium heat. Add the rice wine and a little salt, cover and simmer the chicken over low heat for about 10 minutes.

**2** Meanwhile, wash the bean sprouts. In a separate saucepan, bring ½ litre water to the boil. Add the bean sprouts and cook in the briskly boiling water for a few seconds, then remove them from the pan, drain, and arrange on a plate.

**3** Remove the cooked chicken breast from the water and leave it to cool for about 10 minutes. When cool enough to handle, cut the chicken into very thin shreds about 5 cm long and place them in a large mixing bowl.

**4** To make the sauce, mix the mustard with the soy sauce, vinegar and sesame oil. Pour the sauce over the shredded chicken and mix thoroughly.

**5** Arrange the chicken on the bed of bean sprouts on the plate. Slice the carrot, if using, then use a cutter to cut out flower shapes. Garnish the chicken with the shapes, and serve.

**Variation:** The chicken breast can be fried instead of simmered. Cut the meat into thin strips about 5 cm long, mix with 1 tsp cornflour and 1 tbsp water and fry in hot vegetable oil for about 2 minutes. Season with 1 tbsp dark soy sauce, 1 tbsp rice wine and a little salt.

# Chicken with noodles

*Easy • Summer dish*  **Huang gua fen pi ban ji si**  *Serves 2*

**200 g skinned, boneless chicken breast**
**1 tsp rice wine**
**salt**
**20 g cellophane noodles**
**½ cucumber**

**For the sauce:**
**2 tbsp sesame paste**
**1½ tsp hot soy sauce (see Note)**
**1 tbsp sesame oil**

**Preparation time: 30 minutes**

**1,000 kJ/240 calories per portion**

**1** Bring about ½ litre water to the boil in a small saucepan over medium heat. Add the chicken breast, rice wine and a little salt. Reduce the heat to low, cover the pan and simmer the chicken for about 10 minutes.

**2** Meanwhile, soak the cellophane noodles in hot water for 10 minutes. Wash the cucumber half, cut it in half lengthwise and scrape out the seeds. Cut the halves into pieces about 8 cm long and then lengthwise into thin slices. Arrange the sliced cucumber on a serving plate. Remove the noodles from the water, cut into pieces about 10 cm long and arrange them on top of the cucumber slices.

**3** Remove the chicken from the pan, wrap in foil *(see Note)* and leave to cool for about 10 minutes. When cool enough to handle, cut it into very thin shreds about 3 cm long and arrange them on top of the cellophane noodles.

**4** To make the sauce, mix the sesame paste with 2 tsp water, then stir in the soy sauce and sesame oil. Pour the sauce over the chicken and stir well.

**Note:** If you cannot get hot soy sauce, mix 2 tbsp light soy sauce with ½ tsp *sambal oelek* (available in jars). The chicken will be more succulent if you wrap it in aluminum foil while it is cooling.

# Cellophane noodles

Cellophane noodles are fine, almost transparent noodles, usually made from mung bean starch, but broad bean or pea starch is sometimes used. Those made from mung bean starch are the best quality.

They come in various shapes, from the thin ones added to soup to the wide leaf-shaped noodles, known as *fen pi*. The best-known ones come from Longkou in the province of Shandong. These noodles are very fine and do not stick together.

They are easily digestible and are a popular ingredient in vegetarian cuisine. They are also used in vegetable and meat dishes, soups and salads. Finely chopped, they can be used as a filling for *baozi* (yeast pastry pockets).

Cellophane noodles are available from Chinese grocers and many larger supermarkets. Be careful you do not confuse cellophane noodles with rice noodles which look very similar. Cellophane noodles are sold dried and must be soaked in warm water for about 10 minutes before use.

# Spicy bamboo shoots

*Easy • Winter dish* **La dong sun** *Serves 4*

**400 g canned bamboo shoot pieces**
**1 spring onion**
**1 thin slice fresh ginger root**
**20 g medium-hot red chili peppers**
**(see Glossary)**
**2 tbsp vegetable oil for frying**
**1 tbsp rice wine**
**salt**
**sugar**
**10 cl vegetable stock**
**1 tsp sesame oil**

**Preparation time: 20 minutes**

**400 kJ/95 calories per portion**

**1** In a saucepan, bring ½ litre water to the boil. Add the bamboo shoot pieces and cook in the briskly boiling water for about 1 minute. Remove them from the water with a slotted spoon, drain, then leave to cool. Meanwhile, trim, wash and finely chop the spring onion. Peel and finely chop the ginger.

**2** Cut the bamboo shoots lengthwise into slices about 5 mm thick, then cut again into slices about 5 cm long and 2 cm wide. Wash the red chili peppers, then cut crosswise into thin rings.

**3** Heat the vegetable oil in a wok or frying pan over medium heat for about 3 minutes. Add the spring onion, ginger and chili peppers, and fry them briefly. Add the bamboo shoots. Season with the rice wine and a little salt and sugar, then stir in the stock.

**4** Simmer the mixture, uncovered, over low heat for about 5 minutes, until all the liquid has evaporated. Sprinkle with the sesame oil and serve at once.

**Drink:** Lager is a very good choice to serve with this dish.

**Note:** The Chinese use fresh winter bamboo shoots for this dish, but, unfortunately, they are only available canned in Britain. Before use, they need to be cooked briefly in briskly boiling water to remove the slightly sour flavour.

If you prefer a less fiery version of this dish, remove the seeds from the chili peppers before adding them to the frying pan.

# Glazed walnuts

*Simple • Sweet*   **Liu li tao ren**                                    *Serves 2*

250 g shelled walnuts
½ litre vegetable oil for frying
1 tsp sesame oil
125 g sugar

**Preparation time: 30 minutes**

**5,100 kJ/1,200 calories per portion**

**1** Soak the shelled walnuts in a bowl of hot water for about 10 minutes. Drain and peel away the skins, then pat dry.

**2** Heat the vegetable oil in a wok over medium heat. When hot, carefully add the walnuts and stir-fry until golden. Using a slotted spoon, remove the walnuts and drain on paper towels. Pour off the fat remaining in the wok.

**3** Gently warm the sesame oil in the wok over low heat. Add the sugar and stir until lightly browned.

**4** Remove the wok from the heat and stir the walnuts into the sugar. Remove the walnuts one at a time from the wok, using a spoon or chopsticks. Leave to cool briefly, then serve on a plate.

**Variation:** You can also simmer the walnuts, uncovered, in a saucepan with the sugar and ¾ litre water over low heat for about 15 minutes. When all the liquid has evaporated and the walnuts are coated with a thin layer of sugar, fry them in oil over medium heat until golden. This method of preparing the walnuts takes a little longer.

# Marbled eggs

*Easy • Savoury*    **Cha ye dan**

*Serves 6 to 8*

*10 eggs*
*2 tsp green tea leaves*
*1 piece star anise*
*1 cinnamon stick (about 7 cm long)*
*1 tbsp dark soy sauce*
*salt*

*Preparation time: 5 minutes*
*(plus 45 minutes' cooking time and*
*cooling time)*

*440 kJ/100 calories per portion*
*(if serving 8)*

**1** Boil the eggs in a saucepan with enough water to cover over medium heat for about 10 minutes. Rinse in cold water, then tap lightly all over to crack the shells (the more cracks the better).

**2** Put 1 litre water into a saucepan and add the eggs, tea leaves, star anise and cinnamon stick. Season with the soy sauce and a little salt. Bring the water to the boil, then simmer over low heat for about 45 minutes.

**3** Remove the pan from the heat and leave the eggs to cool in the spicy tea. Shell them just before serving. The eggs can be picked up in the hand and eaten whole. Alternatively, slice or cut them into quarters so that they can be eaten with chopsticks.

**Note:** Marbled eggs get their name because they look like marble when shelled after cooking in the tea. They are also known as tea leaf eggs. They taste even better if left to stand in the tea overnight in the refrigerator.

Even more famous are pine blossom eggs *(ng hua dan)*, also called lime eggs. These are fresh duck eggs, pickled in a mixture of lime, salt, tea leaves and ash for between 15 and 30 days. The egg whites turn brown and the yolks, rather softer than the whites, are dark green. In the West they are inaccurately called "thousand-year-old eggs" or "rotten eggs".

# Spicy mushrooms

*Quick • Special occasion*    **Lu xiang gu**

*Serves 4*

*80 g dried Chinese black*
*mushrooms, preferably of equal size*
*1 spring onion*
*1 thin slice fresh ginger root*
*salt*
*1 tbsp rice wine*
*1 tsp sesame oil*

*Preparation time: 25 minutes*

*190 kJ/45 calories per portion*

**1** Soak the dried mushrooms in warm water for about 10 minutes, then wash them and remove the stalks. Trim and wash the spring onion, and cut it into pieces about 5 cm long. Peel the slice of ginger.

**2** Bring ½ litre water to the boil in a saucepan. Add the spring onion, ginger, salt, rice wine and mushrooms. Simmer over low heat for about 5 minutes.

**3** Remove the mushrooms, ginger and spring onion from the pan, and arrange on a serving plate. Sprinkle the sesame oil over the top and serve at once.

**Variation:** Dried Chinese black mushrooms go very well with bamboo shoots. Prepare 50 g dried mushrooms as described in the recipe. Briefly cook 100 g canned bamboo shoot pieces in briskly boiling water, then cut into thin slices about 3 cm long and 1.5 cm wide. Heat 2 tbsp vegetable oil in a wok over medium heat. Briefly stir-fry the mushrooms and bamboo shoots. Season them with 1 tbsp dark soy sauce, salt and little sugar. Add 10 cl water and simmer, covered, over low heat for about 5 minutes. Meanwhile, mix 1 tsp cornflour with 1 tbsp water. Add to the vegetables and cook briefly, stirring constantly.

# Hot Chinese cabbage

**La bai cai**

**1 kg Chinese cabbage**
**80 g salt**
**10 medium-hot chili peppers**
**(see Glossary)**
**3 tbsp sesame oil**
**10 Sichuan peppercorns**
**80 g sugar**
**2 tbsp white rice vinegar**

**Preparation time: 45 minutes**
**(plus 12 hours' marinating time)**

**460 kJ/110 calories per portion**
**(if serving 6)**

**1** Cut off the tender top part of the Chinese cabbage (this can be used for another dish). Slice the remaining crunchy stalks lengthwise into strips about 2 cm wide, then crosswise into 10 cm wide pieces. Wash the cabbage, drain thoroughly, then layer it in a large salad bowl, sprinkling each layer generously with salt. Leave to stand for about 4 hours.

**2** Remove the cabbage from the bowl, rinse off the remains of the salt with cold water, then squeeze out the liquid with your hands. Return the cabbage to the salad bowl.

**3** Wash the chili peppers, slit them open and remove the seeds, then cut the flesh into thin shreds. Sprinkle the

shreds of about seven chili peppers over the cabbage stalks.

**4** Heat the sesame oil in a small pan over low heat. Add the rest of the chili peppers and the Sichuan peppercorns, and stir-fry for about 1 minute. Strain the oil and pour it over the cabbage.

**5** In a bowl, mix together the sugar, rice vinegar and ½ litre water. Stir thoroughly, then pour the mixture over the cabbage stalks, so that they are covered with the dressing. Cover and leave to marinate for about 8 hours.

**6** Before serving, take the cabbage out of the dressing, cut into pieces about 5 cm long and arrange on a serving plate.

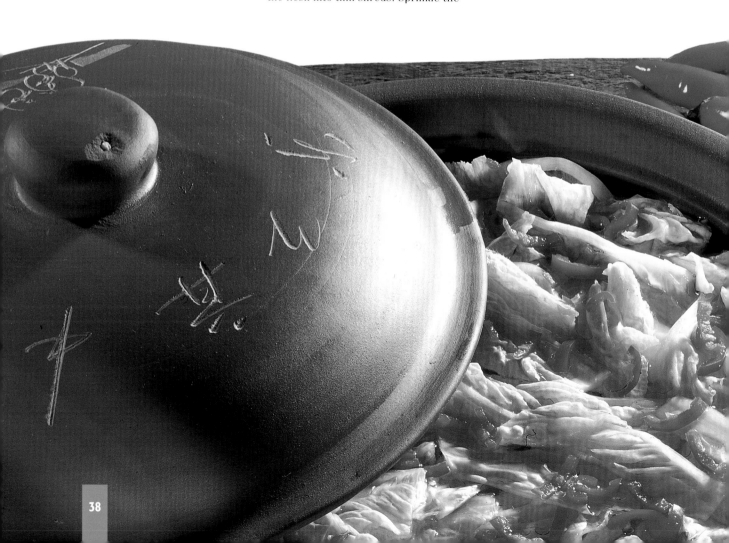

# Chinese cabbage

Chinese cabbage, also known as Chinese leaves, is a large cabbage that looks like a tightly-packed Cos lettuce with crinkled, pale green leaves. It is a delicious vegetable with a mild but distinctive flavour.

Called *da bai cai* (big white cabbage) in Chinese, it is one of northern China's most important winter vegetables. The best of the different varieties come from the province of Shandong and from the area around the city of Tianjin.

Chinese cabbage is good steamed, fried or marinated—on its own or with salt and other ingredients—or served in a salad. It blends well with meat or tofu, and finely chopped it is used to fill pasta pockets.

A great advantage of Chinese cabbabe is that it can be stored: kept in a cool, dry cellar it will last for at least two or three months. In the cities, where the houses have no cellars, the cabbage is stored on the balconies. In order to have enough to see them through the winter, people in northern China buy huge quantities at bargain prices in late autumn.

Cabbage has been eaten in China for 7,000 years. Today, it is a basic ingredient in both everyday and festive meals. In Britain, Chinese cabbage is widely available in larger supermarkets and greengrocers.

# POULTRY AND MEAT

B y far the most famous northern Chinese dish is Peking duck, but there are many other ways of preparing duck. It can be steamed, roasted or braised in rice wine. The same goes for chicken, whose delicate flavour is highly appreciated in China. In fact, no festive Chinese meal is complete without a poultry dish.

In China as a whole, pork is the most widely used meat. It is available in nearly every region at any time of year, and can be combined with almost any other ingredients.

In the north beef is eaten far more frequently than in other regions. Less well-known are the area's exquisite lamb specialities. In the pre-Christian era, only the rich and powerful were able to enjoy lamb and mutton. Fortunately, things have changed since then, and lamb has become one of the region's favourite meats.

The reason for lamb's rise in popularity is threefold. Firstly, northern China's nearest neighbour is Mongolia, where lamb and mutton have always been popular, typically cooked in a firepot or grilled. Secondly, many Muslims, whose religion does not permit them to eat pork, live in northern China. Finally, classic dietary theory classifies lamb as "warming", making it a perfect food for the cold days of late autumn and winter.

# Peking duck

**Beijing kao ya**

*Takes time • Special occasion*

*Serves 4*

**1 oven-ready duck (about 2 kg),
with undamaged skin
30 g maltose or clear honey**

**For the pancakes:
200 g plain flour
4 tbsp vegetable oil**

**For the sauce:
2 bunches spring onions
4 tbsp yellow bean paste or hoisin
sauce**

**Preparation time: 2 hours
(plus 10 hours' drying time)**

**5,000 kJ/1,200 calories per portion**

**1** Wash the duck inside and out, and sew up the body cavity with kitchen twine. Massage the duck thoroughly to separate the skin from the flesh, then make a hole in the neck large enough to insert the nozzle of a bicycle pump. Slowly pump in enough air to separate the skin from the flesh all over the bird *(above)*.

**2** Bring plenty of water to the boil in a large saucepan. Add the duck and boil for about 5 minutes. Remove the duck from the water and dry thoroughly.

**3** Mix the maltose or honey with 10 to 20 cl water to make it easy to spread. Coat the duck with half the maltose or honey solution, then hang it by the neck from a meat hook to dry in a cool place for 1 hour. Spread with the rest of the maltose or honey and hang up to dry for a further 9 hours.

**4** Preheat the oven to 200°C (400°F or Mark 6). Place the duck, breast side upwards, on a grid over a roasting pan. Roast in the centre of the oven for about 45 minutes, then turn it over and continue to roast for a further 30 to 40 minutes, until the duck skin is a lovely reddish brown.

**5** Meanwhile, make the pancakes. In a bowl, mix the flour with about 10 cl lukewarm water. Knead to a smooth, workable dough, then cover with a damp cloth and leave to rest for about 10 minutes. Trim and wash the spring onions, and cut them first into pieces about 10 cm long, then into thin strips. Set aside.

**6** Shape the dough into a roll about 2.5 cm in diameter, then cut the roll into 16 pieces. Brush each piece with oil then, using a rolling pin, roll out to thin pancakes about 15 cm in diameter. Brush a frying pan lightly with oil. Fry the pancakes one at a time over low heat for about 2 minutes on each side. Keep the cooked pancakes warm over a spirit lamp or on a hotplate.

**7** Remove the duck from the oven. Detach the crispy skin and cut it into pieces. Detach the meat from the bone and carve diagonally into small slices.

**8** At the table, lay the pancakes on the plates one at a time. Top with a little duck skin and meat and some spring onion, spread with a little yellow bean paste or hoisin sauce, then roll up and eat with the fingers.

# Duck parcels

**He ye ya zi**

*Serves 6*

*1 oven-ready duck (about 1.5 kg)*
*1 spring onion*
*1 walnut-sized piece fresh ginger root*
*36 g dried or bamboo or lotus leaves (see Note)*
*100 g round-grain rice*
*1 piece star anise*
*4 Sichuan peppercorns*
*2 tbsp rice wine*
*salt*
*3 tbsp dark soy sauce*
*1 tbsp sugar*
*1 tbsp yellow bean paste*

*Preparation time: 1½ hours*

*2,700 kJ/640 calories per portion*

**1** Wash the duck inside and out and pat dry. Cut off the wings, make a deep incision along the back and detach the meat from the bones. Cut the meat into pieces about 5 cm long and 2.5 cm wide, giving about 12 pieces. Trim and wash the spring onion. Peel the ginger. Shred the spring onion and ginger.

**2** Soak the leaves in warm water for about 10 minutes. Meanwhile, stir-fry the rice, star anise and peppercorns in a dry frying pan over medium heat, until they give off a spicy aroma. Leave to cool, then grind coarsely in a mill or crush, using a pestle and mortar.

**3** Mix the duck with the rice wine, salt, soy sauce, sugar, spring onion, ginger and yellow bean paste. Leave to stand for about 5 minutes, then stir in the ground rice and blend thoroughly.

**4** Remove the leaves from the water and drain. Trim off the tips.

**5** Lay three leaves on a work surface so that they overlap. Place a piece of duck with a little ground rice on the leaves *(above)*.

**6** Roll up the leaves, then fold over the left and right edges to make a small parcel. Tie the parcel securely with string or kitchen twine.

**7** Repeat the process with the rest of the leaves and duck *(above)*.

**8** Place all the parcels in a bamboo steamer and replace the lid. Pour water into a saucepan to a level of 4 to 5 cm. Set the steamer over the pan and steam over high heat for about 30 minutes, adding more water to the pan, if necessary. (*See Note, page 50,* if you do not have a bamboo steamer.)

**9** Serve the duck in the parcels and let your guests undo their own parcels at the table.

**Note:** Traditionally, in China, the duck is wrapped in fresh lotus leaves or bamboo leaves. Fresh lotus leaves are not available in Britain, but you can use dried lotus leaves, which are sold in packages in Oriental food stores. The dried leaves must be soaked in warm water for about 20 minutes to soften them before use. They give the food a lovely flavour but are not eaten. If necessary, you can use foil instead.

# Duck with fu zhu

**Hui ya ding fu zhu**

*Serves 2*

*25 g fu zhu (see box, opposite)*
*200 g skinned duck breast*
*2 tbsp cornflour*
*salt*
*rice wine*
*50 g canned bamboo shoot pieces*
*50 g fresh mushrooms*
*1 spring onion*
*1 thin slice fresh ginger root*
*3 tbsp neutral-flavoured*
*vegetable oil*
*1 tsp light soy sauce*
*½ litre chicken stock*
*1 tsp sesame oil*

*Preparation time: 45 minutes*

*1,700 kJ/400 calories per portion*

**1** Soak the *fu zhu* in warm water for about 20 minutes. Meanwhile, wash the duck breast, pat dry and cut into 2 cm cubes. Mix the cornflour with 4 tbsp water. Mix the diced duck with 1 tbsp of the cornflour solution, a little salt and a dash of rice wine.

**2** Bring some water to the boil in a saucepan. Add the bamboo shoots and cook in the briskly boiling water for about 1 minute. Remove from the pan, drain, and leave to cool. Cut into cubes the same size as the meat.

**3** Trim and wash the mushrooms and cut into pieces of similar size to the duck and bamboo shoots. Trim, wash and finely chop the spring onion. Peel and finely chop the ginger. Remove the *fu zhu* from the water and cut into 2 cm pieces.

**4** Heat a wok or frying pan over medium heat. Add the vegetable oil and heat, then briefly stir-fry the spring onions and ginger. Add the duck, stir-fry for about 2 minutes, then add the *fu zhu*, bamboo shoots and mushrooms. Season with salt, soy sauce and 1 tbsp rice wine. Pour in the chicken stock. Bring to the boil, then simmer, covered, over low heat for about 3 minutes. Add the rest of the cornflour solution and stir thoroughly to bind the sauce. Sprinkle the sesame oil over the top and serve at once.

**Note:** This dish looks very pretty garnished with sweet pepper cut into decorative shapes. You can use a special cutter to make a dragon shape, for example.

# Fu zhu

*Fu zhu* is the skin of dried soya bean curd, which is sold in thin, flat sheets or rolled-up sticks. Its high vegetable protein content makes it extremely nutritious and, like tofu (bean curd), it is very popular in vegetarian cookery. It also combines well with other ingredients, particularly meat and vegetables.

Using *fu zhu* and tofu, expert chefs in vegetarian restaurants in Peking can conjure up all kinds of different specialities that look remarkably like poultry dishes, or even resemble a whole duck or chicken. The flat sheets are ideal for making *fu zhu* roulades, which can be filled with minced meat or a mixture of very finely chopped vegetables, according to taste.

Before use, the sheets, or the sticks broken into small pieces, must be soaked for about 20 to 30 minutes, preferably in warm water.

In Britain today, you can buy *fu zhu* in almost any specialist Oriental food shop.

# Crispy fried duck

*Takes time • Peking*

**Xiang su ya zi**

*Serves 4*

*1 oven-ready duck (about 1.5 kg)*
*salt*
*1 tbsp dark soy sauce*
*1 tbsp rice wine*
*1 spring onion*
*1 walnut-sized piece fresh*
*ginger root*
*2 pieces star anise*
*1 piece cinnamon stick, about*
*4 cm long*
*6 to 7 Sichuan peppercorns*
*1.5 litres vegetable oil for*
*deep-frying*
*strips of sweet red pepper for*
*garnish (optional)*

*Preparation time: 45 minutes*

*4,300 kJ/1,000 calories per portion*

**1** Wash the duck inside and out, pat dry, and place in a large fireproof dish which will fit in a bamboo steamer. Rub the duck with salt and soy sauce, and sprinkle with rice wine.

**2** Trim and wash the spring onion, peel the ginger and finely shred both. Add the star anise, cinnamon stick and the shredded spring onion and ginger to the duck. Place the dish in the steamer and close the lid.

**3** Bring 1.5 litres water to the boil in a large saucepan or wok. Set the steamer on top of the pan and steam the duck over high heat for about 30 minutes. (*See Note, page 50,* if you do not have a bamboo steamer.)

**4** Meanwhile, crush the peppercorns, using a pestle and mortar, and mix them with a little salt in a small bowl.

**5** Remove the duck from the steamer and leave to drain. Heat the oil in a wok over high heat, until bubbles rise from a wooden chopstick dipped in the oil. Add the duck to the oil and cook for about 3 minutes, until the skin is crisp, then remove it from the oil.

**6** Carve the duck into joints and serve with the salt and Sichuan peppercorn mixture as a dip. Garnish with strips of sweet pepper, if liked.

**Variation:** Before steaming the duck, rub it inside and out with crushed Sichuan peppercorns and salt. Leave to stand for about 2 hours before adding the ingredients listed above and placing the dish in the steamer. After steaming, remove all the seasoning ingredients, then brush the duck with soy sauce. Leave it to dry briefly, before deep-frying as above.

# Chicken with walnuts

*Simple • Winter dish*

**Jiang bao ji pu ding he tao**

*Serves 4*

*300g chicken breast skinned*
*and boned*
*2 tsp cornflour*
*1 egg white*
*2 tbsp rice wine*
*100 g shelled walnuts*
*5 tbsp vegetable oil*
*1 tbsp yellow bean paste*
*(about 20 g)*
*30 g sugar • 1 tbsp salt*

*Preparation time: 30 minutes*

*1,700 kJ/400 calories per portion*

**1** Cut the chicken into 5 mm cubes and mix with the cornflour, egg white and 1 tbsp of the rice wine. Break the walnuts into halves or quarters, if liked.

**2** Heat a wok or small frying pan and add 4 tbsp of the oil. Add the walnuts and stir-fry over medium heat for about 2 minutes. Remove the walnuts from the pan with a slotted spoon and set aside. Add the chicken breast cubes to the oil remaining in the pan and stir-fry for about 2 minutes. Using a slotted spoon, remove the chicken and reserve.

**3** Add the rest of the oil to the wok. Add the bean paste and heat through over low heat for 1 minute, stirring constantly. Add the sugar, salt and the remaining rice wine, and heat through briefly. Add the chicken pieces and the walnuts, and stir thoroughly for about 1 minute. Garnish with a carrot carved into a flower shape, if liked, and serve at once.

**Variation:** Instead of the yellow bean paste, substitute any fine-textured soy bean paste of your choice.

# Shandong chicken

**Shandong shao ji**

*Takes time • Spicy*

*Serves 4*

*1 oven-ready chicken (about 1 kg)*
*2 spring onions*
*50 g fresh ginger root*
*1 bunch coriander*
*1 small sweet green pepper*
*(about 50 g)*
*20 cl dark soy sauce*
*12 cl plus 1 tsp rice wine*
*100 g sugar*
*2 cinnamon sticks (about*
*7 cm each)*
*4 pieces star anise*
*1 litre vegetable oil*
*1 tbsp light soy sauce*
*salt*
*5 cl chicken stock*
*1 tsp black rice vinegar*
*1 tsp sesame oil*

*Preparation time: 1 hour*
*(plus cooling time)*

*2,200 kJ/520 calories per portion*

**1** Wash the chicken inside and out, then place in a stockpot or fireproof casserole. Cover with boiling water and cook, covered, for about 10 minutes.

**2** Trim and wash the spring onions; finely chop one and reserve it for the sauce. Cut the other one into pieces about 10 cm long. Peel the ginger. Finely chop about 20 g and reserve for the sauce. Slice the rest to add to the stock. Wash the coriander and shake it dry, then chop finely. Wash the sweet pepper, cut in half, remove the core and seeds, and chop finely.

**3** Remove the chicken from the pot. Using a slotted spoon, skim the surface of the stock to remove the scum, then add the dark soy sauce, the 12 cl rice wine, the sugar, cinnamon sticks, star anise, long pieces of spring onion and the sliced ginger.

**4** Bring the stock to the boil, return the chicken to the pot, cover and simmer over low heat for about 15 minutes. Remove the chicken from the pot, leave it to drain, then pat dry.

**5** Heat the vegetable oil in a wok over high heat, until small bubbles rise from a wooden chopstick dipped in the hot oil. Deep-fry the chicken in the hot oil for about 2 minutes.

**6** Remove the chicken from the wok, allow to cool, then carve the chicken, including the bones, into pieces about 5 cm long and 2 cm wide. Drain off the oil from the wok and rinse out the wok with water.

**7** Arrange the chicken pieces in a fireproof dish that fits into a bamboo steamer. Pour over 4 tbsp of the seasoned stock. Stand the dish in the bamboo steamer and replace the lid.

**8** Bring ½ litre water to the boil in a saucepan or wok. Stand the steamer on top of the pan and steam the chicken for about 10 minutes. (If you do not have a bamboo steamer, *see Note.*)

**9** To make the sauce, mix the sweet pepper, coriander, chopped spring onion, chopped ginger, light soy sauce, salt, chicken stock, 1 tsp rice wine, rice vinegar and sesame oil in a bowl.

**10** Serve the chicken pieces and sauce separately. Dip the chicken pieces in the sauce before eating.

**Note:** If you do not have a bamboo steamer, or cannot find one of the correct size, you can arrange the meat on a fireproof dish or plate, cover with a lid and place it on a large metal vegetable steamer attachment. Stand or suspend it over a pot or wok filled with water. You can also stand a heat-resistant cup in a suitable pot. Add about 5 cm water to the pot, stand the plate of meat on the cup, cover, and steam over high heat. Add more water as necessary.

**Variation:** Instead of chicken, you can use poussins for this dish.

# Chicken with chestnuts

*Easy • Autumn dish*  **Li zi men ji**  *Serves 4*

*1 oven-ready chicken (about 1 kg)*
*1 spring onion*
*2 thin slices fresh ginger root*
*3 tbsp vegetable oil*
*2 tbsp rice wine*
*4 tbsp dark soy sauce*
*1 tbsp sugar*
*salt*
*30 cl chicken stock*
*200 g sweet chestnuts*
*250 g broccoli*

*Preparation time: 50 minutes*

*1,900 kJ/450 calories per portion*

**1** Wash the chicken inside and out, then detach the meat from the bones and cut it into 3 cm cubes. Trim, wash and finely chop the spring onion. Peel and finely chop the ginger.

**2** Heat 2 tbsp of the oil in a wok over medium heat for about 3 minutes. Add the spring onion and ginger and stir-fry briefly. Add the chicken and stir-fry over high heat for about 5 minutes. Stir in the rice wine, soy sauce, sugar and a little salt, and continue to stir-fry for a further minute. Add the chicken stock. Bring to the boil, then cover the wok and simmer the chicken over low heat for about 15 minutes.

**3** Meanwhile, make cross-shaped incisions in the tops of the chestnuts.

Bring a saucepan of water to the boil, add the chestnuts and boil over medium heat for about 5 minutes. Rinse them in cold water and peel. Add to the chicken and cook for about 5 minutes.

**4** Wash the broccoli and cut the florets into 5 cm pieces. Bring ½ litre water to the boil in a saucepan. Add the broccoli, the remaining 1 tbsp oil and a little salt. Blanch in the briskly boiling water for about 1 minute, then remove from the pan and drain well. Arrange on a round serving plate.

**5** Remove the chicken from the wok and place it on the bed of broccoli. Arrange the chestnuts around the chicken and spoon 3 to 4 tbsp of the sauce over the top (this should be most of the sauce).

# Spicy chicken wings

*Easy • Shandong* **Ma la ji yi** *Serves 2*

**12 chicken wings**
**1 spring onion**
**2 thin slices fresh ginger root**
**25 g Sichuan peppercorns**
**2 sprigs fresh coriander**
**4 tbsp vegetable oil**
**2 tbsp sugar**
**4 tbsp dark soy sauce**
**salt**
**3 dried chili peppers (see Glossary)**
**1 tsp cornflour**

**Preparation time: 40 minutes**

**2,600 kJ/620 calories per portion**

**1** Wash the chicken wings and trim 4 to 5 cm from the tips. Place the wings in a saucepan with ½ litre water and bring to the boil. Simmer, uncovered, over low heat for a further 10 minutes.

**2** Meanwhile, trim and wash the spring onion and cut into pieces about 5 cm long. Peel the ginger. Place the peppercorns in a muslin bag and tie it up firmly. Wash the coriander, shake dry and chop finely, then set aside. Remove the chicken wings from the pan and drain them. Reserve 10 cl of the cooking liquid.

**3** Heat the oil in a wok over medium heat. Add the sugar and stir until it turns brown. Add the soy sauce and a little salt, cover the wok for a few seconds, then add the chicken stock,

ginger, spring onion, peppercorns, dried chili peppers and the chicken wings. Bring to the boil, reduce the heat and simmer, uncovered, over low heat for about 15 minutes, stirring from time to time.

**4** When only a little liquid remains in the wok, discard the ginger, spring onion and the bag of peppercorns. Mix the cornflour with 2 tbsp water, stir into the ingredients in the wok, and return briefly to the boil. Transfer the chicken wings to a serving plate and sprinkle with the chopped coriander. Serve at once.

**Drink:** A cool lager is excellent for toning down the fiery flavour of this chicken dish.

# Chicken with mushrooms

**Simple • Winter dish**    **Qing zheng dong gu ji**    *Serves 4*

*1 oven-ready chicken (about
1.25 kg)*
*70 g dried Chinese black
mushrooms*
*1 spring onion*
*2 thin slices fresh ginger root*
*salt*
*2 tbsp rice wine*

*Preparation time: 30 minutes
(plus 1 hour's cooking time)*

*1,400 kJ/330 calories per portion*

**1** Wash the chicken well, drain and cut along the back. Place in a saucepan or stockpot with 1 litre water, bring to the boil and simmer, covered, over medium heat for about 15 minutes.

**2** Meanwhile, soak the mushrooms in warm water for about 10 minutes. Trim and wash the spring onion and cut into pieces about 5 cm long. Peel the ginger. Remove the mushrooms from the soaking water and cut any large ones in half.

**3** Remove the chicken from the pan and reserve the stock. Lay the chicken, breast downwards, in a fireproof dish that will fit in a bamboo steamer.

**4** Add the mushrooms, spring onion and ginger to the chicken, and season with a little salt and the rice wine. Strain ¾ litre of the chicken stock through a fine sieve and pour it over the chicken. Cover the dish with foil and stand it in the bamboo steamer.

**5** Bring 1.5 litres water to the boil in a saucepan large enough to hold the bamboo steamer. Stand the steamer on the pan and replace the lid. Steam the chicken for about 1 hour. (*See Note, page 50,* if you do not have a bamboo steamer.) Discard the spring onion and ginger before serving. You can bring the whole chicken to the table, or, if you prefer, carve it beforehand.

## Shiitake mushrooms

Shiitake mushrooms, also known as donggu mushrooms, translates as "winter mushrooms". Due to their exquisite aroma, they are also called *xianngu* (fragrant) mushrooms.

They are an extremely popular ingredient in Chinese cuisine. The meaty flesh has a full-bodied flavour that blends well with poultry, meat or vegetables. They are particularly popular in vegetarian dishes. They can be sautéed, grilled or baked.

The mushrooms are rich in the B-group vitamins, and are reputed to strengthen the body's natural immunity against disease, and so are regarded as an effective means of preventing and treating cancer.

Shiitake mushrooms are cultivated on the trunks of oak and shii trees and picked by hand. They can be bought fresh or dried. In general, fatter mushrooms are of better quality than thin ones. The dried mushrooms, usually called dried Chinese black mushrooms, have a stronger flavour than fresh ones and will keep for three to four months. They need to be soaked in warm water for about 10 minutes before use.

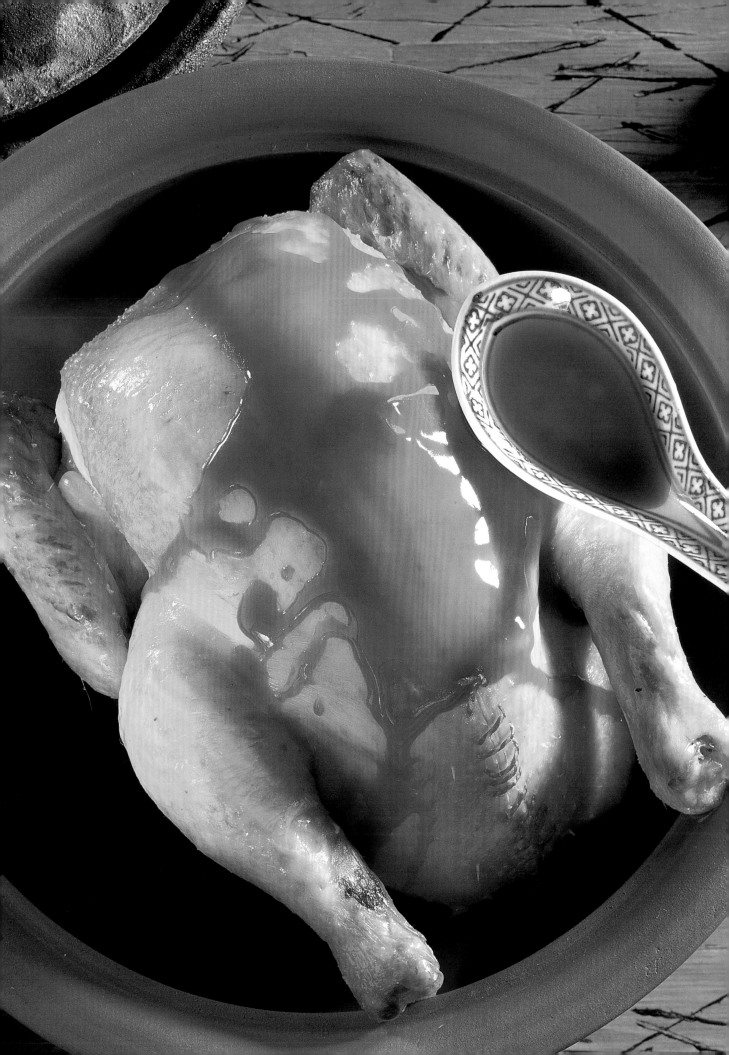

# Ba bao chicken

**Ba bao quan ji**

*Takes time • Festive*

*Serves 4*

1 oven-ready roasting chicken
(about 1.25 kg)
20 cl chicken stock
80 g long-grain rice
20 g dried Chinese black
mushrooms
25 g dried lotus seeds (see
Glossary)
20 g dried red Chinese dates
20 g canned bamboo shoot pieces
25 g sweet chestnuts
25 g ginkgo nuts (see Note
and Glossary)
25 g mild raw ham
2 tbsp vegetable oil
1 heaped tbsp sugar
rice wine
dark soy sauce
salt
1 tsp cornflour

Preparation time: 1 hour
(plus 1 hour's cooking time)

1,900 kJ/450 calories per portion

**1** Wash the chicken inside and out, and pat dry. Bring the stock to the boil in a large saucepan or stockpot. Add the rice and simmer it over low heat for about 10 minutes, then pour the rice into a sieve set over a bowl to reserve the stock. Let the rice drain.

**2** Meanwhile, soak the mushrooms in warm water for about 10 minutes, then wash and cut into 7 mm cubes. Soak the lotus seeds in a separate bowl of warm water for about 10 minutes and remove the green shoots.

**3** Wash and stone the dates and cut into small pieces. Blanch the bamboo shoots for 1 minute in briskly boiling water, drain, then cut into 7 mm dice. Shell the chestnuts and ginkgo nuts. Chop the ham into 3 mm pieces.

**4** Heat a wok over medium heat. Add the oil and heat for about 3 minutes. Add the mushrooms, lotus seeds, dates, bamboo shoots, chestnuts, ginkgo nuts and ham, and stir-fry for 2 minutes.

**5** Add the rice, season with the sugar, 2 tbsp rice wine, 1 tbsp soy sauce and a little salt. Stir thoroughly to mix.

**6** Stuff the chicken cavity with the rice mixture and sew up the body cavity firmly with kitchen twine *(above)*.

**7** Place the chicken, breast upwards, in a dish to fit a bamboo steamer. Cover the dish with foil. Bring 1.5 litres of water to the boil in a saucepan. Place the steamer on top of the pan, cover and steam the chicken for about 1 hour. (*See Note, page 50,* if you do not have a bamboo steamer.)

**8** Remove the dish with the chicken from the steamer. Pour the liquid from the dish into a pan. Add the reserved stock and bring to the boil. Season with a little salt, and a dash of rice wine and soy sauce. Dissolve the cornflour in 2 tbsp water and stir it into the stock. Return to the boil and pour it over the chicken. Bring the chicken to the table whole to serve, or, if you prefer, carve beforehand.

**Variation:** You can also roast the chicken in the oven at 200°C (400°F or Mark 6) for 40 minutes.

**Note:** Red, or Chinese, dates are actually jujubes, olive-shaped fruit also grown in Mediterranean countries. Usually dried in the sun, they are used in sweet Chinese dishes, and as a remedy in traditional Chinese medicine.

*Ba bao*, which translates as "eight delicacies", usually consists of special ingredients not used every day. If you cannot find ginkgo nuts, use the same quantity of walnuts.

Serve the chicken with fragrant rice. Its delicate aroma will add extra flavour to the chicken.

# Chicken with black beans

**Easy • Peking**    **Jiang ya dou chi ji**    *Serves 4*

*400 g skinned and boned chicken breasts*
*75 g fresh ginger root*
*1 spring onion (about 10 cm long)*
*50 g fermented black beans*
*30 cl chicken stock*
*1 tbsp rice wine*
*1 tbsp sugar*
*1 tsp dark soy sauce*
*1 tbsp cornflour*
*salt*
*3 tbsp vegetable oil for frying*
*1 carrot for garnish (optional)*

**Preparation time: 30 minutes**

**99 kJ/240 calories per portion**

**1** Wash the chicken breasts, pat them dry and cut into 2 cm cubes. Peel and thinly slice the ginger. Trim, wash and finely chop the spring onion. Finely chop the fermented black beans.

**2** In a bowl, mix together the chicken stock, spring onion, rice wine, sugar, soy sauce, cornflour and a little salt to make a sauce.

**3** Heat a wok or frying pan, add the oil and heat for 3 minutes over medium heat. Stir-fry the chicken and chopped black beans for about 2 minutes, then add the ginger and the sauce. Cover the wok and simmer the mixture over low heat for about 2 minutes, until the sauce thickens. If using the carrot, cut it into eight slices and use a cutter to create decorative shapes, such as flowers. Garnish the chicken with the carrot shapes and serve at once.

**Note:** The authentic Chinese recipe uses boned meat from a whole chicken, but as skinned and boned chicken breasts are so widely available it is much easier to use them.

When buying fresh ginger look for young roots, as ginger root gets more fibrous as it ages.

58

# Fermented black beans

Fermented black beans—*dou chi* in Chinese—are soya beans preserved with salt and spices. They have a distinctive salty taste, and are used mainly as a seasoning for poultry, meat and fish dishes. Because of their strong flavour, they should be used sparingly.

To produce the fermented beans, soya beans are first soaked, then steamed. They are then mixed with a fermenting agent and a little flour, poured into containers and left for three to four days. Salt and soy sauce are stirred in and the beans are then stored for two to three months in sealed jars. Finally the beans are air-dried. Some beans are fermented without salt or soy sauce for use as a remedy in traditional Chinese medicine.

Fermented beans are available in cans or dried, usually in plastic bags. They will keep for months, even years, refrigerated in tightly sealed jars. Rinse the beans before use and chop them, if wished.

# Poussin with red pepper

*Easy • Shandong*    Chao la zi ji    *Serves 2*

*1 oven-ready poussin (about 400 g)*
*1 sweet red pepper*
*3 tbsp vegetable oil for frying*
*2 tsp dark soy sauce*
*1 tsp rice wine*
*salt*

*Preparation time: 20 minutes*

*1,400 kJ/330 calories per portion*

**1** Wash the poussin inside and out and pat dry. Trim off the wing tips and chop the poussin, including the bones, into 2 cm cubes.

**2** Wash and halve the sweet pepper, remove the core and seeds, then cut the flesh into 2 cm pieces.

**3** Heat the oil in a wok over medium heat. Add the poussin and stir-fry for about 5 minutes, then mix in the soy sauce and rice wine. Season to taste with salt.

**4** Stir-fry for about 1 minute, then add the sweet pepper. Continue to stir-fry for a further 2 minutes, then serve.

**Variation:** For extra flavour, add 30 g dried Chinese black mushrooms. Soak them in warm water for 10 minutes, then drain and chop finely. Add them to the poussin at the same time as the sweet pepper.

If you find eating meat on the bone too fiddly, you can use 300 g chicken breast, but the flavour is quite different. Before frying, cut it into 2 cm cubes and mix with 1 tsp cornflour and 1 tbsp water.

# Chicken with pineapple

*Easy • Sweet-and-sour*    Bo luo ji pian    *Serves 2*

*300 g skinned and boned chicken breast*
*2 egg whites*
*1 tbsp cornflour*
*1 tbsp rice wine*
*1 tsp sugar*
*salt*
*3 tbsp vegetable oil*
*1 can unsweetened pineapple chunks (125 g drained weight)*

*Preparation time: 20 minutes*

*1,500 kJ/360 calories per portion*

**1** Wash the chicken breast, pat dry and cut into thin slices about 4 cm long and 2 cm wide. Mix the slices with the egg whites and cornflour. In a separate bowl, mix together the rice wine, sugar and a little salt to make a sauce.

**2** Heat a wok or frying pan over medium heat, pour in the oil and heat for about 3 minutes. Add the chicken and stir-fry for 2 to 3 minutes. Drain the pineapple chunks and add them to the chicken. Pour in the sauce and briskly stir-fry for about 1 minute.

**Note:** In China, young sugar pea leaves are added to this dish (as in the photograph). If you are lucky enough to be able to obtain some, take 200 g young sugar pea leaves, trim, wash and drain them. Add them to the chicken with the pineapple. Young sugar pea leaves not only taste good, but they make a lovely colour contrast with the other ingredients.

# Firepot

**Shuan yang rou**

*1 kg lean shoulder of lamb*
*(about 2 cm thick)*
*25 g dried Chinese black*
*mushrooms*
*80 g cellophane noodles*
*250 g Chinese cabbage*

*For the sauce:*
*2 tbsp fermented tofu (see Note)*
*2 tbsp sesame paste*
*½ tsp chili oil*
*2 tbsp sesame oil*
*10 cl light soy sauce*
*1 bunch coriander*
*1.5 to 2 litres chicken stock*

*Preparation time: 1 hour*
*(plus 2 hours' chilling time)*

*1,300 kJ/310 calories per portion*
*(if serving 6)*

**1** To make it easier to cut, chill the lamb in the freezer compartment of the refrigerator for about 2 hours, then cut into paper-thin strips about 5 cm long. Arrange the strips on serving plates.

**2** Meanwhile, soak the dried black mushrooms in a bowl of warm water for about 10 minutes. Place the cellophane noodles in another bowl, cover with hot water and leave them to soak for about 10 minutes. Trim and wash the Chinese cabbage leaves and pat dry with paper towels. Cut into strips about 8 cm long and 3 cm wide and arrange on plates.

**3** Mix the tofu with the sesame paste, chili oil, sesame oil and soy sauce, and divide it between several bowls. Wash the coriander, shake dry and tear off the leaves. Chop them finely and divide between several small bowls.

**4** Remove the cellophane noodles from the water, cut in half and arrange on several plates. Drain the mushrooms, remove the stalks, cut the caps in half, wash, pat dry and add to the stock for the firepot. Bring the stock to the boil in a saucepan on the cooker, then pour into the firepot. Heat the firepot.

**5** At the table, everyone selects their own ingredients and then cooks them in a little wire mesh spoon in the hot stock for 1 to 2 minutes before dipping them in the sauce and eating. The coriander leaves can be eaten with the other ingredients or on their own. In China, the lamb is eaten first, followed by the mushrooms, cellophane noodles and Chinese cabbage.

**Note:** Traditional Chinese firepots are available in Britain from Oriental food stores, complete with little wire mesh spoons for cooking the ingredients in the hot stock. Alternatively, a fondue set that includes fondue forks or chopsticks makes a perfect substitute. In China, this dish is served in winter, since the Chinese believe that lamb provides the body with plenty of heat.

Ordinary tofu is not suitable for this dish, so if you cannot find fermented tofu, omit it and add only 4 tbsp soy sauce. In Peking, salted chive flowers are used in the sauce,

but these are rarely available in this country. If you are able to find Chinese chives (*jiu cai*), finely chop 50 g and add them to the sauce. Chinese pancakes *(see Steps 5 and 6, page 42)* are very good with a firepot meal, or you can serve thin baguettes.

**Variation:** Fish, prawns, chicken and tofu or a selection of vegetables can all be prepared for cooking in a firepot.

# Lamb with sesame seeds

*Easy • Peking* **Zhi ma yang rou**                    *Serves 2 to 3*

**300 g boned leg of lamb**
**1 spring onion**
**1 walnut-sized piece fresh**
**ginger root**
**2 tbsp rice wine**
**salt**
**freshly ground white pepper**
**2 egg whites**
**3 tbsp cornflour**
**4 eggs**
**½ litre vegetable oil for frying**
**50 g white sesame seeds**

**Preparation time: 40 minutes**

**2,900 kJ/690 calories per portion**
**(if serving 3)**

**1** Wash the leg of lamb, pat dry, then mince or chop very finely. Wash, trim and finely chop the spring onion. Peel and finely chop the ginger.

**2** Mix the minced lamb, spring onion, ginger and rice wine in a bowl. Season to taste with salt and pepper, and leave to marinate for about 10 minutes. Meanwhile, in another bowl, thoroughly mix the egg whites and cornflour.

**3** Break the whole eggs into a bowl and whisk them, adding a little salt. Heat a frying pan over low heat and brush with a little oil. Pour half the beaten egg into the pan and tilt the pan so that the egg spreads very thinly over the base. Fry over low heat for 3 to 4 minutes, until the omelette is set.

**4** Remove from the pan, and repeat the process with the remaining beaten egg. Leave the omelettes to cool on a plate.

**5** Divide the lamb into 2 or 3 portions, shaping each one into a strip about 12 cm long, 6 cm wide, and 1.5 cm thick. Wrap an omelette around each portion *(above)*, then brush all over with the egg white and cornflour batter.

**6** Sprinkle the sesame seeds evenly over each parcel, pressing the seeds gently into the omelette *(above)*. Each parcel must be coated as thickly as possible with sesame seeds.

**7** Heat the oil in a frying pan over medium heat, until small bubbles rise from a wooden chopstick dipped in the hot fat. Slide the lamb parcels carefully into the oil. Fry over medium heat for about 3 minutes, then turn carefully and fry on the other side for a further 3 minutes, until crisp and golden.

**8** Remove the parcels from the pan with a slotted spoon, and drain off the fat. Before serving, cut each parcel in half crosswise and again lengthwise.

**Variation:** Use minced pork instead of lamb for the filling.

# Barbecued lamb

*Simple • Peking*  **Kao yang rou chuan**  *Serves 4*

500 g boned leg of lamb (about
2 cm thick)
2 spring onions
1 walnut-sized piece fresh
ginger root
2 garlic cloves
2 tbsp rice wine
2 tbsp light soy sauce
1 tsp sesame oil
salt

**Preparation time: 45 minutes**

**1,400 kJ/330 calories per portion**

**1** Cut the lamb into thin slices about 3 cm long and 2 cm wide. Trim and wash the spring onions and cut them into pieces about 3 cm long. Peel and thinly slice the ginger and garlic.

**2** Mix the lamb with the spring onions, ginger, garlic, rice wine, soy sauce and sesame oil. Season with a little salt and leave to marinate for about 30 minutes. Meanwhile, prepare the barbecue.

**3** Thread the lamb on to skewers, alternating with pieces of spring onion, ginger and garlic. Grill on the barbecue for about 3 minutes on each side.

**Drink:** Serve the kebabs with a dry rosé de Provence or lager.

**Variation:** Instead of marinating the lamb with the ingredients given in the recipe, thread the meat straight on to the skewers and grill them over the charcoal. As it cooks, brush the meat first with soy sauce, and then with a mixture of 6 to 7 crushed Sichuan peppercorns, 1 tsp hot paprika and a little salt. Finally, sprinkle both sides with sesame oil. If a barbecue is not practical, cook the lamb under a preheated grill.

# Lamb with leeks

**Quick • Winter dish**   **Cong bao yang rou**                                  *Serves 2*

**300 g boned leg of lamb (about
2 cm thick)
1 tbsp dark soy sauce
2 tbsp rice wine
2 tsp sesame oil
200 g leeks
2 garlic cloves
4 tbsp vegetable oil
salt
1 tsp dark rice vinegar**

**Preparation time: 30 minutes**

**2,500 kJ/600 calories per portion**

**1** Cut the lamb across the grain into thin slices about 5 cm long and 2 cm wide. Mix the meat with half the soy sauce, half the rice wine and half the sesame oil.

**2** Trim and wash the leeks, and cut at a slight angle into pieces about 2 cm wide. Peel and finely crush the garlic.

**3** Heat a wok or frying pan, then pour in the vegetable oil and heat it over medium heat for about 3 minutes. Add the crushed garlic and fry briefly.

**4** Add the meat and stir-fry briefly over high heat, then add the rest of the soy sauce and rice wine. Add a little salt and continue to stir-fry for a further 1 minute. Add the leeks and stir-fry for about 30 seconds longer. Sprinkle with the vinegar and the rest of the sesame oil. Stir thoroughly and serve at once.

**Note:** This dish is very popular in Peking in the winter. It must be cooked very quickly and stir-frying should not take more than 2 minutes, otherwise the meat will be tough.

**Variation:** Spring onions can be used instead of leeks.

# Hot and spicy beef

**Quick • Summer dish**   **Sheng jian niu liu**   *Serves 2 to 3*

*400 g beef fillet*
*1 spring onion*
*1 thin slice fresh ginger root*
*2 tsp rice wine*
*1 tbsp hot soy sauce (see Note)*
*1 tbsp sesame oil*
*salt*
*freshly ground black pepper*
*1 egg*
*2 garlic cloves*
*2 tbsp cornflour*
*3 tbsp vegetable oil for frying*
*1 tsp sugar*

**Preparation time: 30 minutes**

**1,400 kJ/330 calories per portion (if serving 3)**

**1** Wash the meat, pat dry, and cut into slices about 2 cm thick *(above)*. Trim, wash and finely chop the spring onion. Peel and finely chop the ginger.

**2** Mix the beef slices in a bowl with the spring onion, ginger, half the rice wine, half the hot soy sauce, half the sesame oil and a little salt and pepper. Leave to marinate in a cool place for about 5 minutes.

**3** Meanwhile, in another bowl, whisk the egg with 2 tbsp water. Peel and crush the garlic cloves.

**4** Put the cornflour in a bowl. Heat a frying pan over medium heat, then add the oil. After about 3 minutes, when the oil is hot, remove the pan from the heat. Coat a piece of meat in cornflour then dip it in the beaten egg *(above)*.

**5** Place the coated piece of meat in the frying pan, then repeat the process with the rest of the meat.

**6** When all the meat is in the frying pan, return the pan to the heat and fry over medium heat, until the slices are golden on both sides. Remove the meat from the frying pan and pour off the remaining oil.

**7** Add the rest of the sesame oil and the garlic to the pan, fry briefly over low heat, then add the rest of the rice wine and hot soy sauce, the sugar, and a little salt.

**8** Return the meat to the pan and fry over medium heat for about 2 minutes, turning the slices two or three times. Serve at once.

**Drink:** Serve with a cool lager.

**Note:** If your local Oriental shop does not stock hot soy sauce, you can mix 1 tbsp light soy sauce with a dash of chili oil or ½ tsp *sambal oelek* (hot chili relish, available in jars).

# Fried fillet of beef

**More complex • Peking**  **Gan bian niu rou si**  *Serves 2*

**250 g beef fillet**
**30 g celery**
**1 spring onion**
**2 thin slices fresh ginger root**
**6 Sichuan peppercorns**
**2 tbsp vegetable oil**
**salt**
**½ tsp hot bean paste**
**1 tbsp soy sauce**
**sugar**
**1 tbsp rice wine**
**1 tbsp dark rice vinegar**

**Preparation time: 30 minutes**

**1,000 kJ/240 calories per portion**

**1** To make it easier to slice the fillet of beef really thinly, place it in the freezer for about 2 hours. Slice the chilled beef thinly across the grain, then into thin shreds about 5 cm long.

**2** Trim and wash the celery and the spring onion, and cut them both into pieces about 3 cm long. Cut each piece lengthwise into halves or thirds, if liked. Peel and finely shred the ginger. Using a pestle and mortar, crush the Sichuan peppercorns.

**3** Heat the oil in a wok or frying pan over high heat for about 3 minutes. Add the beef and stir-fry briskly, then add a little salt. When the meat is brown, add the hot bean paste, soy sauce, rice wine and a little sugar, and stir-fry for a further 2 to 4 minutes.

**4** When almost all the liquid in the wok has evaporated, stir in the celery, then the spring onion and ginger. Sprinkle with the rice vinegar and stir-fry for another 30 seconds.

**5** Transfer the meat to a serving plate, discarding the celery and spring onion. Sprinkle the crushed peppercorns over the top and serve at once.

# Braised belly of pork

**Not difficult • Many regions**  **Kou rou**  **Serves 4**

**500 g boned belly of pork, in one piece, with rind (see Note)**
**salt**
**rice wine**
**2½ tbsp dark soy sauce**
**1 spring onion**
**1 walnut-sized piece fresh ginger root**
**200 g broccoli**
**1 litre vegetable oil for deep-frying**
**2 pieces star anise**
**1 cinnamon stick (about 7 cm long)**
**1 tsp sugar**
**carrot slices for garnish (optional)**

**Preparation time: 1 hour**

**2,800 kJ/670 calories per portion**

**1** Bring ½ litre water to the boil in a small saucepan, add the meat, a little salt and a dash of rice wine. Cover and cook over medium heat for 20 minutes. Remove the meat from the pan; reserve the stock. Allow the meat to cool a little and then brush with 1 tbsp soy sauce. Leave to stand for about 5 minutes.

**2** Meanwhile, trim and wash the spring onion and cut into pieces about 10 cm long. Peel and thinly slice the ginger. Wash the broccoli and divide it into small florets.

**3** Heat the oil in a wok over high heat until small bubbles rise from a wooden chopstick dipped in the hot oil. Add the meat and deep-fry for about 3 minutes, turning it once. Remove the meat from the pan and return it to the stock.

**4** Spread the spring onion, ginger, star anise, cinnamon stick and sugar on top of the meat, then pour over 2 tbsp rice wine and the rest of the soy sauce. Simmer, covered, over low heat for about 20 minutes. At the end of the cooking time, discard the spring onion, ginger, star anise and cinnamon. Remove the meat from the pan and leave to cool slightly.

**5** Blanch the broccoli in a saucepan in enough briskly boiling water to cover for about 3 minutes, drain, and season with a little salt.

**6** Place the meat, rind downwards, on a chopping board and cut into slices about 1.5 cm thick. Arrange on a plate, surrounded by the broccoli florets, and pour 2 to 3 tbsp sauce over the meat. Garnish with carrot slices cut into decorative shapes, if liked, and serve.

**Note:** The pork is particularly tasty if it is cooked with the rind on.

# Pork with almonds

*Takes time • Peking*

**Xing he rou**

*Serves 4*

**100 g whole shelled almonds**
**500 g boned belly of pork, about**
**4 cm thick, with rind**
**1 spring onion**
**1 thin slice fresh ginger root**
**1 tbsp vegetable oil**
**2 tbsp brown sugar crystals**
**1 tbsp rice wine**
**2 tbsp dark soy sauce**
**2 tsp cornflour**

**Preparation time: 1½ hours**

**2,900 kJ/690 calories per portion**

**1** Soak the almonds in hot water for about 10 minutes. Meanwhile, cut the belly of pork into 4 cm cubes. Trim and wash the spring onion and cut it into pieces about 10 cm long. Peel the ginger. Remove the almonds from the water, peel off the skins and then tie the almonds in a small muslin bag.

**2** Heat the oil in a wok over low heat. Add the sugar and stir until dissolved. Add the meat and stir-fry over medium heat for about 3 minutes until browned. Add the spring onion, ginger, rice wine, soy sauce, almonds and ½ litre water. Bring to the boil, cover and simmer over low heat for about 50 minutes.

**3** Remove the wok from the heat and remove the bag of almonds. Open it and pour the almonds into a round fireproof dish, at least 5 cm deep and 20 cm in diameter. Arrange the belly of pork, rind downwards, on top, and pour over 3 to 4 tbsp of the stock. Place the dish in a large saucepan and pour in water to a level of about 4 cm water. Cover the meat and steam for 15 minutes.

**4** Just before the end of the cooking time, bring the stock remaining in the wok to the boil. Dissolve the cornflour in 1 tbsp water and stir it into the stock to bind it. Remove the dish of meat from the saucepan, place an upturned plate on top, and turn the meat out on to the plate. Pour the sauce over the meat and almonds, and serve.

**Drink:** Serve the pork with a cold beer.

# Sweet-and-sour pork

*Easy • Summer dish*

**Tang cu li ji**

*Serves 2*

**300 g lean pork**
**1 egg white**
**3 tsp cornflour**
**salt**
**1 spring onion (about 10 cm long)**
**1 thin slice fresh ginger root**
**2 tbsp sugar**
**1½ tsp dark rice vinegar**
**1 tbsp rice wine**
**1 tbsp dark soy sauce**
**½ litre plus 1 tbsp vegetable oil**
**tomato cut into flower shape for**
**garnish (optional)**

**Preparation time: 30 minutes**

**2,500 kJ/600 calories per portion**

**1** Wash the meat, pat dry, and cut into pieces about 3 cm long and 2 cm wide. Place the pieces in a bowl.

**2** Mix the egg white with 2 tsp of the cornflour and a little salt, then stir the mixture into the meat.

**3** Trim, wash and finely chop the spring onion. Peel and finely chop the ginger. Mix the sugar, vinegar, rice wine, soy sauce, spring onion, ginger, a little salt and the rest of the cornflour in a bowl to make a sauce.

**4** Heat the wok over medium heat, then add the ½ litre oil. When the oil is hot, add the meat, a piece at a time, and fry until golden. Remove the meat from the wok with a slotted spoon and drain off the fat. Pour away the oil in the wok.

**5** Heat 1 tbsp fresh oil in the wok over medium heat. Pour in the prepared sauce and bring to the boil, stirring constantly. When the sauce thickens, return the meat to the wok, stir thoroughly and return to the boil. Only boil very briefly, otherwise the crisp coating on the meat will go soggy and loose its tangy flavour.

**6** If liked, garnish with a tomato cut into a flower shape. Serve at once.

# Fried pork

**Jiang bao bai rou si**

*Not difficult • Autumn dish*

*Serves 2 to 3*

**300 g lean pork**
**1 small sweet green and 1 small**
**sweet red pepper (about 50 g each)**
**1 tbsp yellow bean paste**
**1 tbsp rice wine**
**salt**
**2 tbsp flour**
**½ litre vegetable oil for frying**
**1 tbsp dark soy sauce**
**1 tsp sugar**
**freshly ground white pepper**
**1 tsp sesame oil (optional)**

**Preparation time: 45 minutes**

**1,600 kJ/380 calories per portion**
**(if serving 3)**

**1** Wash the meat. Bring ½ litre water to the boil in a small saucepan. Add the meat, cover and boil over medium heat for about 5 minutes. Meanwhile, wash and halve the peppers, remove the core and seeds and shred thinly.

**2** Remove the meat from the pan, leave to cool, then cut into strips about the thickness of a chopstick. Mix the bean paste, rice wine and a little salt in a bowl, and stir in the meat strips. Sift the flour on to a plate and coat the meat in the flour.

**3** Heat the ½ litre oil in a wok or frying pan over high heat until small bubbles rise from a wooden chopstick dipped in the hot oil. Fry the meat in batches for about 2 minutes, until golden.

**4** Remove the meat strips from the pan and drain off the oil on them. Pour off the oil in the wok, leaving just a thin film in the bottom.

**5** Return the meat to the wok, add the shredded peppers and stir thoroughly. Add the soy sauce, sugar and a little white pepper, and stir-fry over high heat for about 1 minute. Serve at once, sprinkled with sesame oil, if liked.

**Note:** The meat must be boiled first, otherwise it will not be crisp.

# Pork fillet with coriander

*Quick • Piquant*     **Yan bao li ji**                                    *Serves 2*

**200 g pork fillet**
**1 tsp cornflour**
**1 egg white**
**salt**
**5 sprigs coriander**
**1 spring onion**
**1 thin slice fresh ginger root**
**1 garlic clove**
**3 tbsp vegetable oil**
**10 cl meat stock**
**1 tbsp rice wine**
**freshly ground white pepper**
**1 tsp sesame oil**
**1 yellow pepper for garnish**
**(optional)**

**Preparation time: 30 minutes**

**1,500 kJ/360 calories per portion**

**1** Cut the pork fillet into thin strips about 5 cm long. Dissolve the cornflour in 3 tbsp water. Mix the meat with the egg white, the cornflour solution and a little salt. Wash the coriander, shake dry and cut into pieces about 3 cm long. Trim, wash and finely chop the spring onion. Peel and finely chop the ginger. Peel the garlic and cut it into thin strips.

**2** Heat the vegetable oil in a wok over high heat and stir-fry the pork for about 30 seconds until the pieces no longer stick together, then remove them from the wok. Stir-fry the spring onion, ginger and garlic in the oil remaining in the wok over medium heat for about 1 minute, then add the stock, rice wine, coriander, salt, a little pepper and the

meat. Bring quickly to the boil over high heat, then immediately remove from the heat.

**3** Sprinkle the meat with the sesame oil and serve garnished with yellow pepper cut into decorative pig shapes, if liked.

**Variation:** Instead of coriander, you can use a sweet green pepper (about 100 g). Cut it into thin strips and stir-fry with the spring onion, ginger and garlic for about 1 minute. Add the other ingredients and the fried meat, and proceed as above.

# Pork balls

Si xi wan zi

*300 g lean belly of pork*
*30 g canned bamboo shoot pieces*
*1 spring onion*
*1 piece fresh ginger root (about*
*1.5 cm long and 1.5 cm thick)*
*6 Sichuan peppercorns*
*salt*
*3 tbsp cornflour*
*3 tbsp dark soy sauce*
*1 tbsp rice wine*
*1 egg*
*1 egg white*
*½ litre plus 1 tbsp vegetable*
*oil for frying*
*200 g Chinese cabbage leaves*
*40 cl meat stock*

*Preparation time: 1 hour*

*2,100 kJ/500 calories per portion*

**1** Mince or finely chop the pork. Blanch the bamboo shoots in briskly boiling water for about 1 minute, remove from the water, drain and chop finely.

**2** Trim and wash the spring onion. Peel the ginger, then finely chop both spring onion and ginger. Crush the Sichuan peppers using a pestle and mortar.

**3** Mix the meat, bamboo shoots, spring onion, ginger, a little salt, 2 tbsp of the cornflour, 2 tbsp of the soy sauce, the rice wine and the whole egg. Using your hands, shape the mixture into four balls *(above)*. In a separate bowl, mix the rest of the cornflour with the egg white.

**4** Heat the ½ litre oil in a wok or pan over high heat. Dip the pork balls in the egg white and cornflour batter. Slide them, one at a time, into the oil and fry for about 2 minutes. Remove the pork balls from the oil with a slotted or wire spoon *(above)* and reserve.

**5** Wash the Chinese cabbage leaves and pat dry. Line a fireproof casserole or stockpot with the cabbage leaves. Arrange the pork balls on top, pour over the stock and the rest of the soy sauce. Cover the casserole or stockpot and bring to the boil over medium heat. Turn the heat down low and simmer for about 15 minutes.

**6** Heat the 1 tbsp oil in a small pan over low heat and stir-fry the crushed Sichuan peppercorns, then strain the pepper-flavoured oil over the pork balls. Serve at once, straight from the casserole or stockpot.

**Drink:** Serve this dish with a dry, highly acidic white wine, such as a Riesling from the Rhineland-Palatinate.

**Note:** In China, these pork balls are traditionally served in an earthenware pot, which, because of its slightly domed base, is only suitable for use over gas. An oven-to-table cast-iron pot is a good substitute.

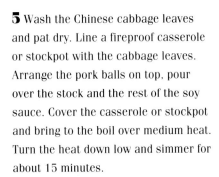

# FISH AND SEAFOOD

**W**riting about fish, the famous gourmet Li Yu (1611–1680) said: "Those who are fond of fish attach the greatest importance to freshness and then to fat content. One can ask no more than that the fish be high in fat and still fresh. Fish with a very fresh flavour is suitable for clear soups, while fatty fish should be finely cut and opulently served. In the preparation of fish, everything depends on the correct exposure to heat. If the fish is cooked too long before eating, the flesh is dead and the flavour lost.

"Fish must be removed from the pot as soon as it is cooked. If it is cooked in advance, all its delicate taste will evaporate. If it is warmed up, it will taste like stale wine or cold rice that has been reheated. It looks the same but the taste is not the same."

Today, the freshness of fish is still the most important consideration. In general, the northern Chinese prefer the delicate flavour of freshwater fish, which are often farmed in the north. Moreover, Chinese dieticians forbid sufferers from certain illnesses to eat fish from the sea.

In the coastal province of Shandong, however, fish and seafood play an important role in the diet. The people of this region could not live without prawns and squid, and carp is also a great favourite.

While we in the West often cook fish with lemon juice, Chinese cooks add a little fresh ginger and rice wine.

# Sizzling rice with prawns

**San xian guo ba**

*Takes time • Special occasion*

*Serves 3 to 4*

150 g round-grain rice
5 dried Chinese black mushrooms
100 g lean pork (about 2 cm thick)
salt
rice wine
100 g raw prawns
2 tbsp cornflour
1 egg white
1 spring onion
1 thin slice fresh ginger root
50 g fresh button mushrooms
½ litre plus 2 tbsp vegetable
oil for frying
30 cl chicken stock
50 g frozen peas
freshly ground white pepper

Preparation time: 40 minutes
(plus up to 12 hours´ drying time)

1,800 kJ/430 calories per portion
(if serving 4)

**1** Put the rice in a pan with ¼ litre water, bring to the boil, then simmer, uncovered, over low heat. Just before all the liquid has evaporated, cover and turn the heat down as low as possible. Simmer for a further 5 minutes.

**2** Leave the rice to cool slightly, then spread on a sheet of greaseproof paper in a layer about 5 mm thick. Leave it to dry in a draughty place for a whole day, or place in the oven at minimum setting for about 30 minutes. When dry, break the rice into fairly large chunks.

**3** Soak the dried mushrooms in warm water for about 10 minutes, then remove them from the water and cut into small pieces. Meanwhile, wash the pork and place it in a saucepan with 30 cl water. Bring to the boil, cover and boil over medium heat for about 5 minutes, adding a little salt and a dash of rice wine. Remove the meat from the pan, allow it to cool, then cut into thin slices about 3 cm long.

**4** Wash and shell the prawns, remove the dark vein-like intestines and pat dry. In a bowl, dissolve the cornflour in about 4 tbsp water. In a separate bowl,

mix together the raw prawns, 1 tbsp rice wine, the egg white, a little salt and ½ tsp of the cornflour solution. Trim, wash and finely chop the spring onion. Peel and finely chop the ginger. Trim, wash and slice the button mushrooms.

**5** Heat the 2 tbsp vegetable oil in a wok over medium heat. Lift the prawns out of the marinade and drain briefly. Stir-fry the prawns in the oil for about 2 minutes, then remove from the pan. Briefly fry the spring onions and ginger in the oil remaining in the pan. Stir in 1 tbsp rice wine and the stock, followed by the soaked black mushrooms and the

button mushrooms, the peas, pork and prawns. Season with 1 tsp rice wine, salt and pepper. Cover and bring to the boil over medium heat. Stir in the rest of the cornflour solution. Return to the boil and stir for 2 to 3 minutes to bind the sauce. Tansfer it to a warmed bowl.

**6** Just before the prawns are ready *(see Note)*, heat the ½ litre oil in a pan over high heat until small bubbles rise from a wooden chopstick dipped in the hot fat. Add the rice chunks and deep-fry for about 30 seconds, until golden. Remove from the oil with a slotted spoon and arrange on a serving plate.

**7** Pour the prawn and pork mixture over the top of the fried rice chunks, and serve at once.

**Note:** When the hot rice chunks come into contact with the prawn mixture, they make a sizzling sound, which is why the dish is known as "sizzling rice". It is best to have the oil already heated on another burner just before the prawn mixture is ready, since this dish should be served immediately.

# Prawns with green pepper

*Quick · Mild*   **Xia ren chao qing jiao**   *Serves 2*

*200 g raw prawns*
*1 tsp rice wine*
*1 egg white*
*1 tsp cornflour*
*salt*
*freshly ground white pepper*
*1 spring onion (about 10 cm long)*
*1 thin slice fresh ginger root*
*1 small sweet green pepper*
*(about 75 g)*
*3 tbsp vegetable oil*

*Preparation time: 25 minutes*

*960 kJ/230 calories per portion*

**1** Wash and shell the prawns, remove the dark vein-like intestines and pat dry, then cut into 2 cm dice. Mix the diced prawns with the rice wine, egg white, cornflour and a little salt and pepper, stirring thoroughly.

**2** Trim, wash and finely chop the spring onion. Peel and finely chop the ginger. Wash the green pepper, remove the core and seeds, then cut the pepper into 2 cm pieces.

**3** Heat the oil in a wok or frying pan over medium heat and briefly stir-fry the spring onion and ginger. When they begin to give off a spicy aroma, remove them from the wok with a spoon, and

discard. Add the prawns to the spicy-flavoured oil and stir-fry for 1 to 2 minutes, then remove from the pan.

**4** Add the chopped pepper to the oil remaining in the pan, season with salt and stir-fry for about 2 minutes. Return the prawns to the pan, mix thoroughly, and serve at once.

**Variation:** If you can find Chinese chives (*jiu cai*, also called garlic chives) in an Oriental food store, use 100 to 150 g instead of the green pepper. They have a stronger, highly aromatic flavour, but are not always available in Britain. You can also use a mix of sweet red and green peppers.

# Prawns in soy sauce

*Easy · Festive*   **Hong shao da xia**   *Serves 2*

*400 g raw prawns*
*1 spring onion*
*1 walnut-sized piece fresh*
*ginger root*
*3 tbsp vegetable oil*
*5 to 6 Sichuan peppercorns*
*1 tbsp rice wine*
*2 tbsp dark soy sauce*
*1 tsp sugar*
*20 cl chicken stock*

*Preparation time: 20 minutes*

*1,400 kJ/330 calories per portion*

**1** Wash the prawns, cut off the feelers, but preferably leave the heads on. Pat dry. Trim, wash and finely chop the spring onion. Peel and finely chop the piece of ginger.

**2** Heat 1 tbsp of the oil in a pan over low heat. Crush the peppercorns with a pestle and mortar, add them to the oil and stir-fry for about 1 minute, then strain and reserve the flavoured oil.

**3** Heat the rest of the oil in a wok or frying pan over medium heat. Briefly stir-fry the spring onion and ginger. Add the prawns and fry until they turn red. Stir in the rice wine and briefly cover the wok.

**4** Stir in the soy sauce and sugar, and pour the stock over the prawns. Bring to the boil, cover the wok and simmer over low heat for about 2 minutes. Sprinkle with the pepper-flavoured oil and serve at once.

**Note:** Shandong province is right on the coast, and both Shandong king prawns and the numerous local ways of preparing them are famous the length and breadth of China.

# Sweet-and-sour carp

**Tang cu li yu**

*More complex · Winter dish*

*Serves 4*

*1 cleaned carp (about 750 g)*
*salt*
*5 to 6 dried wood ear mushrooms*
*1 spring onion*
*1 walnut-sized piece fresh*
*ginger root*
*1 garlic clove*
*100 g carrots*
*1 litre vegetable oil for deep-frying*
*4 tbsp cornflour*
*200 g sugar*
*2 tbsp dark soy sauce*
*5 tbsp dark rice vinegar (see Note)*

*Preparation time: 45 minutes*

*2,700 kJ/640 calories per portion*

**1** Wash the carp inside and out, and pat dry. Using a sharp knife, make crosswise incisions about 3 cm apart and 1 cm deep along both sides of the fish *(above)*, and rub with salt.

**2** Soak the wood ear mushrooms in warm water for about 10 minutes. Meanwhile, trim, wash and finely chop the spring onion. Peel and finely chop the ginger and garlic. Wash and peel the carrots and cut crosswise into 5 cm pieces, then lengthwise into thin strips. Remove the mushrooms from the water, wash thoroughly and cut into small pieces. Preheat the oven to its minimum setting.

**3** Heat the oil in a wok or frying pan over high heat, until small bubbles rise from a wooden chopstick dipped in the hot oil. In a small bowl, dissolve 3 tbsp of the cornflour with 5 tbsp water. Spoon the batter over the carp *(above)* until it is coated, then gently place it in

the hot oil and deep-fry for 4 to 5 minutes, turning it over after 2 minutes. Remove the fish from the wok and keep warm in the oven.

**4** Pour off most of the oil from the wok or frying pan, leaving only a thin film. Briefly stir-fry the spring onion, ginger and garlic over low heat. Add the wood ear mushrooms and carrot strips and continue to stir-fry briefly.

**5** Add the sugar, soy sauce and 20 cl water, followed by the vinegar. Bring to the boil over high heat. Dissolve the rest of the cornflour in 2 tbsp water, then stir it into the sauce. Return the sauce to the boil, then immediately pour it over the fish, and serve. At the table, everyone uses chopsticks to pick off pieces of fish.

**Note:** Chinese vinegar is made from rice and is milder than wine or malt vinegar. It is sold in specialist Oriental food stores.

In China, no festive meal is complete without fish. Since carp is believed to bring good luck, it is the first choice when entertaining guests.

**Variation:** If you prefer not to cook a whole fish, use 300 g fish fillet and cut it into 2 cm cubes. Mix the cubes with 1 tbsp cornflour, 1 tsp rice wine and a little salt, and deep-fry in batches in the hot oil for about 2 minutes. Serve with the sauce as above.

# Braised carp

**More complex • Shandong**  **Gan shao li yu**  *Serves 4*

1 cleaned carp (about 600 g)
100 g rindless, streaky bacon, cut
into 5 mm-thick rashers
1 walnut-sized piece fresh
ginger root
1 spring onion
25 g canned bamboo shoot pieces
3 to 4 tbsp vegetable oil
1 tbsp rice wine
1 tbsp dark soy sauce
1 tsp sugar
salt
1 tsp cornflour
1 tsp sesame oil
carrot and cucumber slices for
garnish (optional)

**Preparation time: 30 minutes**

**1,700 kJ/400 calories per portion**

**1** Wash the carp inside and out, and pat dry. Using a sharp knife, make crosswise incisions about 3 cm apart and 1 cm deep along both sides of the fish *(see Step 1, page 85).*

**2** Remove any gristle from the bacon, then cut into 5 mm dice. Peel the ginger and cut into thin strips. Trim and wash the spring onion, cut crosswise into 1 cm pieces, then lengthwise into thin strips. Bring a saucepan of water to the boil and blanch the bamboo shoots in the briskly boiling water for about 1 minute, then remove from the pan and drain. Leave to cool, then cut into 1 cm dice.

**3** Heat a wok or frying pan over medium heat, then add the vegetable oil. When it is hot, lay the carp in the oil and fry for about 1 minute on each side. Remove the fish from the pan.

**4** Stir-fry the ginger and bacon in the oil remaining in the pan over medium heat for about 1 minute. Add the bamboo shoots and stir briefly. Add the rice wine, soy sauce, sugar and a little salt. Return the carp to the pan, add 30 cl water and bring to the boil. Cover and cook over low heat for 10 minutes. Transfer the carp to a serving dish.

**5** Add the spring onion to the sauce in the pan. If necessary, boil, uncovered, over medium heat to reduce it. Dissolve the cornflour in 3 tbsp water, add it to the sauce, and stir thoroughly. Finally, sprinkle the sesame oil over the sauce and stir thoroughly.

**6** Pour the sauce over the fish. Garnish with slices of carrot and cucumber, if liked, and serve at once. At the table, everyone uses chopsticks to pick off pieces of the fish.

# Trout in vinegar sauce

**Simple • Spring dish**   **Cu jiao yu**   *Serves 2*

*1 cleaned trout (about 500 g)*
*1 spring onion*
*1 walnut-sized piece fresh*
*ginger root*
*1 sprig coriander*
*2 tbsp rice wine*
*salt*
*1 tsp white rice vinegar*
*1 tsp sesame oil*
*freshly ground white pepper*
*carrot slices for garnish*

*Preparation time: 25 minutes*

*1,200 kJ/290 calories per portion*

**1** Wash the trout inside and out, and pat dry. On one side of the fish, using a sharp knife, make crosswise incisions about 4 cm apart and 1 cm deep *(see Step 1, page 85)*. Turn the fish over and make diagonal incisions about 4 cm apart and 1 cm deep on the other side.

**2** Trim and wash the spring onion. Cut it diagonally into pieces about 5 cm long, then lengthwise into thin strips. Peel and shred the ginger. Wash the coriander, shake dry and chop finely.

**3** Bring ¾ litre water to the boil in a wok over medium heat. Add the trout and 1 tbsp rice wine. Cover and simmer over medium heat for about 2 minutes, then remove the fish from the water. Pour off about ½ litre of the stock.

**4** Add the rest of the rice wine, a little salt, the spring onion, ginger and trout to the stock left in the wok. Cover and boil over high heat for about 5 minutes. Transfer the fish to a serving dish.

**5** Add the vinegar, sesame oil, chopped coriander and a little pepper to the sauce, and stir briefly. Pour it over the fish, garnish with carrot slices cut into shapes, if liked, and serve at once.

# Trout with ginger

**Jiang si yu**

*Easy • Tianjin*

*Serves 2*

*1 cleaned trout (about 500 g)*
*1 spring onion*
*1 walnut-sized piece fresh*
*ginger root*
*3 tbsp vegetable oil*
*1 piece star anise*
*4 tbsp rice wine*
*1 litre meat stock*
*salt*
*1 tbsp dark soy sauce*

*Preparation time: 30 minutes*

*1,700 kJ/400 calories per portion*

**1** Wash the trout inside and out, and pat dry. Using a sharp knife, make crosswise incisions about 4 cm apart and 1 cm deep along both sides of the fish *(see Step 1, page 85)*.

**2** Trim and wash the spring onion, cut it diagonally into pieces 5 cm long, and then lengthwise into thin strips. Peel the ginger and cut off three thin slices (about 5 g), then cut the remainder into very thin shreds about 4 cm long.

**3** Heat 1½ tbsp of the oil in a wok over low heat. Briefly stir-fry the star anise and sliced ginger, moisten with 2 tbsp rice wine, then add about 95 cl of the stock. Add the fish and season with

salt. Bring to the boil over high heat, then cook over medium heat for about 5 minutes. Remove the fish from the pan, drain, and transfer to a serving dish. Pour off the stock from the wok.

**4** Heat the remaining 1½ tbsp oil in the wok, briefly stir-fry the shredded ginger over low heat, then add the soy sauce, the remaining 5 cl stock and the rest of the rice wine. Bring the sauce to the boil over high heat, pour it over the fish and serve at once.

**Variation:** This dish can be made with carp instead of trout.

# Fried fish cubes

**Bao yu ding**

*Easy • Shandong*

*Serves 2*

*200 g fish fillets (for example, cod,*
*plaice or perch)*
*2 egg whites*
*2 tbsp plus 1 tsp cornflour*
*2½ tbsp rice wine*
*salt*
*freshly ground white pepper*
*50 g canned bamboo shoot pieces*
*½ spring onion*
*1 garlic clove*
*½ sweet green pepper*
*½ sweet red pepper*
*4 tbsp vegetable oil*
*1 tsp sesame oil (optional)*

*Preparation time: 30 minutes*

*1,500 kJ/360 calories per portion*

**1** Remove any bones from the fish with tweezers, then cut it into 1.5 cm cubes. Mix the fish cubes with the egg whites, the 2 tbsp cornflour, ½ tbsp of the rice wine and a little salt. In another bowl, mix 1 tsp cornflour with 5 cl water and season with salt and pepper. Set aside.

**2** Bring a saucepan of water to the boil, add the bamboo shoots and blanch in the briskly boiling water for about 1 minute, then remove from the water and drain. Leave to cool, then cut into 1.5 cm cubes.

**3** Trim and wash the spring onion and cut into short pieces. Peel and thinly slice the garlic. Wash the green and red pepper halves, remove the cores and

seeds, and cut the flesh into 1.5 cm pieces. Heat the vegetable oil in a wok over medium heat. When the oil is hot, add the fish cubes and stir-fry for about 2 minutes, then remove from the wok.

**4** Add the spring onion and garlic to the oil remaining in the wok and briefly stir-fry over medium heat. Add the bamboo shoots and peppers, and stir-fry for about 1 minute.

**5** Return the fish cubes to the wok and season with the rest of the rice wine. Stir in the cornflour solution. Simmer for about 1 minute, stirring constantly. Sprinkle with the sesame oil, if liked, and serve at once.

# Squid rolls

**Yan bao you yu juan**

*Serves 2*

300 g cleaned squid
2 tsp cornflour
1 spring onion
1 thin slice fresh ginger root
1 garlic clove
4 sprigs coriander
5 cl meat stock
1 tsp rice wine
½ tsp white rice vinegar
salt
freshly ground white pepper
1 tsp sesame oil

**Preparation time: 30 minutes**

**680 kJ/160 calories per portion**

**1** Discard the heads and tentacles of the squid. Wash the pouches and pat dry. Discard the outer skin. Cut open one side of each body pouch. Using a sharp knife, make crosswise incisions on the inside of the pouch about 2 mm apart, cutting halfway through the flesh, then cut into pieces about 5 cm long and 2 cm wide *(above)*.

**2** In a bowl, mix the squid pieces with 1 tsp of the cornflour.

**3** Trim and wash the spring onion. Peel the ginger and garlic. Shred the spring onion and ginger, and thinly slice the garlic. Wash the coriander, shake dry and cut into pieces about 3 cm long.

**4** Bring about ½ litre water to the boil in a pan. Blanch the squid in the briskly boiling water for about 30 seconds: during the blanching process the squid pieces will roll up. The squid should not be cooked for any longer, otherwise it will be tough. Remove it from the water and drain.

**5** Pour the stock into the wok, add the rice wine and vinegar, and season with salt and pepper. Bring to the boil.

**6** Add the shredded spring onion and ginger, the sliced garlic, coriander and drained squid, and return the mixture briefly to the boil.

**7** Dissolve the remaining cornflour in 3 tsp water. Stir the mixture into the boiling stock and return briefly to the boil. Sprinkle with the sesame oil and serve at once.

**Note:** It is important that the squid is carefully cut, following the instructions in Step 1, not just for the sake of appearance but also to achieve the best taste. Cut correctly, the squid absorbs all the flavours of the other ingredients. However, if you find this method too laborious, it can be cut into strips about 5 cm long and 5 mm wide. When buying the squid, bear in mind that the fatter they are, the easier they are to cut.

In China, dried squid is used in this dish as well as fresh squid. The dried squid is soaked for several hours before use. While fresh squid is white, the dried variety is reddish, giving the dish an attractive blend of colours.

Fresh coriander is very sensitive to heat and should only be added at the very end of the cooking time.

# VEGETARIAN DISHES

The traditional Chinese diet is a well-balanced one and, because of the huge variety of vegetables available in China, few nations on earth enjoy more simple and healthy fare than the Chinese.

In a Chinese market, you will find not only vegetables native to China—bean sprouts, cabbage, bamboo shoots and mushrooms—but also others that were once unknown in the country, such as spinach, carrots and tomatoes. Unfortunately, some vegetables, such as young pea leaves, shepherd's purse and taro are difficult, if not impossible, to find in Britain.

The choice of vegetables at mealtimes varies with the changing seasons. Traditional Chinese medicine dictates that food should match the rhythm of nature, and certain vegetables should only be eaten at the appropriate time of year.

The range of vegetables, together with tofu (soya bean curd), lend a quite special appeal to Chinese vegetarian cookery. Tofu is thought to have been invented by nomadic tribes from the north who invaded the Chinese heartland between the sixth and ninth centuries AD. They were accustomed to dairy products made from cows' and goats' milk. Since the local Chinese raised few cattle and knew nothing of dairy products, the newcomers used the readily available soya milk to create tofu.

# Little tofu boxes

**Dou fu xiang zi**

*Serves 4*

*20 g dried Chinese black mushrooms*
*10 g dried tiger lily buds (see page 97)*
*100 g canned bamboo shoot pieces*
*500 g fresh, or vacuum-packed, firm tofu*
*1 spring onion*
*1 thin slice fresh ginger root*
*200 g Chinese cabbage*
*1 egg*
*3 tbsp dark soy sauce*
*2 tbsp rice wine*
*salt*
*freshly ground white pepper*
*1 litre plus 1 tbsp vegetable oil for frying*
*¾ litre vegetable stock*
*few drops sesame oil (optional)*

*Preparation time: 45 minutes*

*1,500 kJ/360 calories per portion*

**1** Soak the mushrooms and tiger lily buds separately in warm water for about 10 minutes. Blanch the bamboo shoots for about 1 minute in briskly boiling water, drain and leave to cool.

**2** Meanwhile, cut the tofu into eight equal pieces and pat dry. Trim, wash and finely chop the spring onion. Peel and finely chop the ginger.

**3** Cut the bamboo shoots lengthwise into thin slices, then lengthwise into strips, and finally crosswise into very small dice. Wash the Chinese cabbage, pat dry, then cut the leaves lengthwise into thin strips, then crosswise into small pieces.

**4** Drain the mushrooms and tiger lily buds, wash thoroughly, and drain them again. Discard the hard stalks of the tiger lily buds. Finely chop the buds and the drained mushrooms.

**5** To make the filling for the tofu boxes, mix the mushrooms, tiger lily buds, bamboo shoots and Chinese cabbage in a bowl. Add the egg, 1 tbsp of the soy sauce, 1 tbsp of the rice wine and a little of the spring onion and ginger. Season to taste with salt and pepper, and stir thoroughly.

**6** Heat the 1 litre oil in a wok over medium heat and deep-fry the tofu for about 7 minutes, until golden on all sides. Using a slotted spoon, remove it from the pan, drain off the fat and leave to cool. Pour off the oil in the wok.

**7** Using a small knife, gently slit open one side of each piece of the fried tofu. Divide the filling into eight portions.

**8** Use a teaspoon to stuff one portion of filling into each piece of tofu *(above)*. If necessary, cut away some of the tofu to make room for the filling. Having been fried, the tofu pieces will be fairly hollow inside, so should be very easy to fill, like little boxes.

**9** Heat the 1 tbsp oil in the wok over medium heat and briefly fry the rest of the spring onion and ginger. Add the tofu boxes and the stock. Season with salt, the remaining soy sauce and the rest of the rice wine. Cook, uncovered, for about 15 minutes. Sprinkle with the sesame oil, if liked, and serve.

**Note:** When tofu is deep-fried like this it develops lots of little holes, which absorb plenty of liquid during the rest of the cooking process, making it very succulent. In markets throughout China, ready-made tofu boxes are sold in different shapes, such as balls or triangles.

If you cannot fit all the filling into the tofu boxes, simply cook what is leftover with the tofu and serve it with them.

# Eggs with mushrooms

*Simple • Summer dish*  **Huang gu mu er chao dan**  *Serves 2 to 3*

**5 medium-sized, dried wood
ear mushrooms
10 g dried tiger lily buds
1 small cucumber (about 250 g)
4 eggs
salt
5 tbsp vegetable oil
10 cl vegetable stock**

**Preparation time: 25 minutes**

**1,100 kJ/260 calories per portion
(if serving 3)**

**1** Soak the wood ear mushrooms and tiger lily buds separately in warm water for about 10 minutes, then drain and wash thoroughly. Cut the mushrooms into strips. Discard the hard stalks of the tiger lily buds and finely chop the buds. Peel the cucumber, cut in half lengthwise, and slice thinly.

**2** Break the eggs into a bowl and whisk with a little salt. Heat 4 tbsp of the oil in a wok or frying pan over medium heat. Pour in the eggs and cook over medium heat until they start to set. Cut the omelette into chunks and continue to cook until they are golden but not dry. Remove the pieces from the pan.

**3** Heat the rest of the oil over medium heat and stir-fry the cucumber slices and chopped mushrooms and tiger lily buds for 1 to 2 minutes. Stir in a little salt and the vegetable stock. Stir in the omelette pieces and return briefly to the boil. Serve at once.

**Variation:** Instead of cucumber and wood ear mushrooms, use tomatoes. Plunge the tomatoes briefly into boiling water, skin and slice them, then stir-fry as described above and mix with the stock and eggs.

# Tiger lily buds

Tiger lily buds are the air-dried and steamed golden buds of the yellow tiger lily. In China, fresh tiger lily buds are readily available, but in Britain only the dried ones are sold in Oriental food stores. In any case, the dried buds have a more intense flavour than the fresh ones, although eating too many of either can give you indigestion.

Because they are long—5 to 7.5 cm—and yellow, tiger lily buds are also known as "golden needles" (*jin zhen cai*). Their delightful musky fragrance and slightly sweet flavour makes them a popular ingredient in Chinese vegetarian cuisine.

Tiger lily buds blend very well with many other ingredients, including tofu (soya bean curd), meat and Chinese cabbage. Finely chopped tiger lily buds, mixed with other vegetables, are used to fill Chinese ravioli (*bao zi*).

Before use, the buds must be soaked in warm water for about 10 minutes. After soaking, the hard stalks should then be removed. The buds should not be cooked for too long, otherwise they will start to fall apart.

# Tofu hotpot

**Sha guo dong dou fu**

*250 g tofu*
*5 medium-sized dried wood ear mushrooms*
*1 spring onion*
*1 thin slice fresh ginger root*
*25 g canned bamboo shoot pieces*
*100 g broccoli*
*100 g button mushrooms*
*2 tbsp vegetable oil*
*40 cl vegetable stock*
*1 tsp rice wine*
*salt*
*freshly ground white pepper*

*Preparation time: 30 minutes (plus 2 hours' freezing time and 1 hour's thawing time)*

*540 kJ/130 calories per portion (if serving 4)*

**1** Place the tofu in the freezer for about 2 hours *(see Note)*, then thaw for 1 hour and cut into 2.5 cm cubes. Bring ¾ litre water to the boil in a pan, add the tofu and blanch in the briskly boiling water for about 1 minute. Remove from the water with a slotted spoon and drain the tofu in a colander.

**2** Meanwhile, soak the dried wood ear mushrooms in warm water for about 10 minutes. Trim, wash and finely chop the spring onion. Peel and finely chop the ginger. Bring some water to the boil in a saucepan. Blanch the bamboo shoots in the briskly boiling water for about 1 minute, then drain and leave to cool. Cut the cold bamboo shoots into 1.5 cm dice. Wash the broccoli and cut the florets into 3 cm pieces. Trim, wash and chop the button mushrooms. Drain the soaked wood ear mushrooms and wash thoroughly.

**3** Heat 1 tbsp of the oil in a wok over medium heat and briefly stir-fry the ginger and spring onion. Add the bamboo shoots, wood ear and button mushrooms, tofu, and stock. Season with the rice wine and a little salt and pepper, and bring to the boil. Transfer the contents of the wok to a clay or other fireproof pot that is suitable for serving, then cover and simmer over low heat for about 15 minutes.

**4** Meanwhile, heat the rest of the oil in a frying pan over medium heat. Stir-fry the broccoli florets for about 2 minutes and season with salt and pepper. Add to the rest of the ingredients in the pot, and serve at once.

**Note:** Freezing creates lots of little holes in the tofu, so that it absorbs the flavour of the mushrooms and all the other ingredients while cooking.

# Tofu with pine nuts

**Song zi dou fu**

*250 g tofu*
*1 sprig coriander*
*2 tbsp vegetable oil*
*50 g pine nuts*
*15 cl vegetable stock*
*1 tbsp rice wine*
*salt*
*freshly ground white pepper*
*1 tsp cornflour*

*Preparation time: 20 minutes*

*1,500 kJ/360 calories per portion*

**1** Wash the tofu and cut into 2.5 cm cubes. Bring ¾ litre water to the boil in a saucepan and blanch the tofu cubes for about 1 minute in the briskly boiling water, then remove from the pan, and drain. Wash the coriander, shake dry, and chop finely.

**2** Heat the vegetable oil in a wok over low heat and stir-fry the pine nuts for about 2 minutes, until they turn brown.

**3** Add the tofu cubes, stock, rice wine and a little salt and pepper and cook the mixture over medium heat for about 1 minute, until heated through.

**4** Dissolve the cornflour in 2 tsp water and stir it into the other ingredients in the wok. Sprinkle with the chopped coriander and serve at once.

# Tofu with leek

*Easy • Shandong*  **Da cong chao dou fu**  *Serves 2*

250 g tofu • ½ leek
3 tbsp vegetable oil
salt • 1 tbsp dark soy sauce
1 tbsp rice wine
15 cl vegetable stock
1 tsp cornflour
1 tsp sesame oil

*Preparation time: 30 minutes*

1,100 kJ/260 calories per portion

**1** Cut the tofu into pieces about 5 cm long, 3 cm wide and 2 cm thick. Trim and wash the half leek, and cut it at a slight angle into pieces about 4 cm long and 2 cm wide.

**2** Pour the vegetable oil into the wok. Lay the tofu pieces side by side in the wok and fry over medium heat for 5 to 6 minutes on each side, until golden. Remove the tofu with a slotted spoon.

**3** Add the leek to the oil remaining in the wok and fry briefly over low heat. Return the tofu to the pan. Season with salt, soy sauce and rice wine, and add the stock. Cook over medium heat for about 2 minutes.

**4** Dissolve the cornflour in 3 tsp water and stir into the stock. Continue to stir to bind the tofu mixture. Sprinkle with the sesame oil and serve at once.

# Sweet-and-sour cucumber

*Quick • Summer dish*  **Tang cu huang gua**  *Serves 4*

500 g cucumber
salt
2 tbsp sugar
2 tsp dark rice vinegar
1 tsp sesame oil

*Preparation time: 20 minutes*

210 kJ/50 calories per portion

**1** Wash the cucumber and cut in half lengthwise. Scrape out the seeds and cut the cucumber crosswise into pieces about 5 cm long and then lengthwise into thin slices.

**2** Sprinkle the cucumber slices with salt, then leave for about 10 minutes to draw off the liquid. Pat dry.

**3** Place the cucumber slices in a bowl, sprinkle the sugar, vinegar and sesame oil over them and stir thoroughly to coat the cucumber. Arrange the slices on a plate and serve at once.

**Note:** For a hot, spicy tang, add 1 tsp chili oil. If you like a sweeter flavour, as they do in China, use 100 g sugar.

# Beans with garlic

*Quick • Summer dish*  **Qing chao dou jiao**  *Serves 2*

300 g runner beans
3 garlic cloves
2 to 3 tbsp vegetable oil
salt • 1 tsp rice wine
15 cl vegetable stock

*Preparation time: 20 minutes*

510 kJ/120 calories per portion

**1** Trim and wash the beans, then cut them diagonally into thin strips. Peel the garlic and cut first into thin slices and then into shreds.

**2** Heat the oil in a wok or frying pan over medium heat. Briefly fry the garlic. Add the beans and continue to stir-fry briefly, then season with a little salt and the rice wine. Add the stock, cover the wok and cook for about 3 minutes, then serve at once.

**Note:** To retain their vitamin content and keep them crisp, the thinly sliced runner beans should only be fried in the oil for a few minutes.

# Braised aubergines

**Simple · Mild**   **Su shao qiezi**                                    *Serves 4*

1 kg medium-sized aubergines
2 spring onions
2 garlic cloves
1 walnut-sized piece fresh ginger
root (about 25 g)
1 sprig coriander
1 litre vegetable oil for frying
2 tsp sugar
3 tbsp dark soy sauce
1 tbsp rice wine
¼ litre vegetable stock
salt

**Preparation time: 40 minutes**

**1,300 kJ/310 calories per portion**

**1** Wash the aubergines, pat dry and cut lengthwise into 1.5 cm-thick slices and then crosswise into pieces about 5 cm long. Trim and wash the spring onions. Peel the garlic and ginger. Finely chop the spring onions, garlic and ginger. Wash the coriander, shake it dry and chop finely.

**2** Heat the oil in a wok over high heat until small bubbles rise from a wooden chopstick dipped in the hot oil. Add the aubergines and fry for about 3 minutes.

**3** Remove the aubergines from the pan with a slotted spoon and drain off the fat. Pour off most of the oil remaining in the wok, leaving only a thin film.

**4** Heat the oil left in the wok over low heat. Add the sugar and stir until it caramelizes. Add the spring onions, ginger and garlic; fry for 1 minute. Lay the aubergines on top of the caramel.

**5** Mix the soy sauce, rice wine, stock and a little salt in a bowl, and pour the sauce over the aubergines. Tilt the wok from side to side to spread the sauce evenly, then cover the wok and simmer for about 3 minutes, until only a little sauce remains. Sprinkle the chopped coriander over the top and serve.

# Silver ears with vegetables

**Yin er su hui**

*Easy • Mild*

*Serves 4*

**10 g dried silver ear mushrooms**
**20 g dried Chinese black mushrooms**
**100 g small button mushrooms**
**100 g carrots**
**100 g broccoli**
**40 cl vegetable stock**
**1 tsp sugar**
**salt**
**1 tbsp cornflour**
**1 tsp sesame oil**

**Preparation time: 40 minutes (plus 1 hour's soaking time)**

**220 kJ/52 calories per portion**

**1** Soak the silver ear mushrooms in warm water for 1 hour. Drain, remove the roots and cut the mushrooms into 2 to 3 cm pieces. Meanwhile, soak the black mushrooms in warm water for about 10 minutes, then wash and cut into pieces the same size as the button mushrooms. Trim and wash the button mushrooms. Peel the carrots. Wash the broccoli. Cut the broccoli florets and the carrots into pieces the same size as the button mushrooms.

**2** Place the silver ears in a saucepan with ½ litre water, cover and simmer over low heat for about 15 minutes. Using a slotted spoon, remove them from the pan and set aside.

**3** Return the water in the pan to the boil and blanch the black and button mushrooms, broccoli and carrots, one after the other, for 1 to 1½ minutes each, adding ¼ litre boiling water as you blanch each vegetable.

**4** Place each type of vegetable in a separate bowl and pour cold water over them to keep them crisp.

**5** Arrange the silver ears in the middle of a serving dish. Remove the black mushrooms, button mushrooms, carrots and broccoli from the water, drain, then arrange in an alternating pattern around the silver ears.

**6** Bring the vegetable stock to the boil in a pan. Add the sugar and season with a little salt. Dissolve the cornflour in 2 tbsp water and stir into the stock. Return to the boil and pour it over the vegetables. Sprinkle with the sesame oil and serve at once.

**Note:** Although this dish may seem bland for European tastes, a less piquant dish of this kind is always included in a large Chinese menu, to ensure harmony of flavours.

# Hot and spicy potatoes

**Simple • Tasty**   **Su chao la tu dou si**   *Serves 2*

**300 g waxy potatoes**
**1 piece each sweet green pepper**
**and sweet red pepper (about**
**25 g each)**
**1 garlic clove**
**4 tbsp vegetable oil**
**2 dried medium-hot chili peppers**
**(see Glossary)**
**10 Sichuan peppercorns**
**1½ tbsp light soy sauce**
**5 tbsp white rice vinegar**
**salt**

**Preparation time: 45 minutes**

**1,100 kJ/260 calories per portion**

**1** Peel the potatoes and cut them into very thin slices. This is easier if you first cut off a piece from one side of each potato so that it rests firmly on the chopping board. Cut the slices into matchstick-sized strips—the thinner the potato sticks, the crisper they will be when cooked.

**2** Rinse the potato strips twice under cold running water, then soak them in cold water for 10 to 15 minutes to remove the excess starch. Meanwhile, wash the pieces of sweet green and red pepper, removing any core or seeds, and cut the flesh into thin strips. Peel and finely chop the garlic. Drain the potato strips.

**3** Heat the oil in a frying pan or wok over a medium heat and stir-fry the chili peppers, Sichuan pepper corns and garlic until they give off a spicy aroma. Strain the flavoured oil into another container, then pour it back into the pan.

**4** Add the potatoes and sweet peppers to the oil, season with soy sauce and briskly stir-fry over high heat for about 3 minutes, until cooked through. Turn the heat right down low, quickly stir in the vinegar, and, if liked, season with a little salt. Serve at once.

**Drink:** The best choice with this spicy potato dish is a cool lager.

**Variation:** Spring onions can be used instead of sweet red and green pepper.

# Fried celery

**Easy • Spring dish**   **Dong gu chao qin cai**   *Serves 2*

**20 g dried Chinese black**
**mushrooms**
**250 g tender celery**
**3 tbsp vegetable oil**
**5 Sichuan peppercorns**
**salt**
**10 cl vegetable stock**

**Preparation time: 20 minutes**

**570 kJ/140 calories per portion**

**1** Soak the dried mushrooms in warm water for about 10 minutes. In the meantime, wash the celery, pat dry and cut the sticks diagonally into pieces about 5 cm long, then lengthwise into thin strips. Remove the mushrooms from the water, wash and remove the stalks, then cut into thin strips.

**2** Heat 1 tbsp of the oil in a small pan over low heat and stir-fry the Sichuan peppercorns for about 1 minute, then strain this flavoured oil into another container, and reserve.

**3** In a wok or frying pan, heat the remaining 2 tbsp vegetable oil over medium heat. Briefly stir-fry the celery and mushrooms, season with salt, and add the stock. Cover and cook over medium heat for about 3 minutes. Do not cook for too long or the celery will lose its bite.

**4** Sprinkle the reserved flavoured oil over the top of the mushrooms and celery, and serve at once.

**Drink:** Serve green tea with this dish.

# Bean sprouts with ginger

*Quick • Summer dish*   **Cu peng lu dou ya**   *Serves 2*

*250 g bean sprouts*
*1 spring onion*
*1 thin slice fresh ginger root*
*2 tbsp vegetable oil*
*1 tsp light soy sauce*
*1 tbsp rice wine*
*1 tsp white rice vinegar*
*salt*

*Preparation time: 15 minutes*

*580 kJ/120 calories per portion*

**1** Wash and drain the bean sprouts. Trim and wash the spring onion and cut them crosswise into pieces 5 cm long, then lengthwise into thin strips. Peel and shred the ginger.

**2** Heat the vegetable oil in a wok over high heat. Briefly stir-fry the spring onions and ginger.

**3** Add the bean sprouts, soy sauce, rice wine and rice vinegar. Season to taste with salt and briskly stir-fry for about 1 minute—the bean sprouts must be cooked very quickly in order to retain their crispness. Remove them from the pan and serve at once.

**Note:** This is an ideal dish for those on a diet, since it is low in calories and easy to digest. When buying bean sprouts, look for white sprouts whose roots are not too long.

**Variation:** A sweet green pepper can be added to this dish. Remove the core and seeds, wash the pepper and cut the flesh into thin strips about 4 cm long. Stir-fry the shredded pepper with the bean sprouts.

## Bean sprouts

Bean sprouts are the young sprouts of mung and other beans.

Beans, especially soya beans, are a very popular ingredient in Chinese cuisine. However, since beans can be rather hard to digest, they are often processed into a variety of other products. Bean sprouts is one such product, and illustrates the inventiveness of Chinese cooks.

There are two basic varieties of bean sprouts: mung bean sprouts (*lu dou ya*) and soya bean sprouts (*huang dou ya*). The most frequently used are mung bean sprouts, though they are sometimes incorrectly labelled as soya bean sprouts. Mung bean sprouts are long and slender, and are widely available fresh in supermarkets. They are delicious served raw as a crunchy salad ingredient on a hot summer day, or they can be briefly fried as a vegetable. They can also be mixed with other ingredients to make a filling for spring rolls, or used to add extra flavour to fried noodles.

Soya bean sprouts are larger than mung bean sprouts and less widely available in shops—though they can be sprouted very easily at home. In China they are only eaten fried.

# SOUPS

If you are invited to a meal in China, you will notice that, contrary to Western custom, soup is served as an in-between course, or more probably at the end of the meal. In ancient China, the arrival of the soup was taken as a sign that the guests should start thinking about taking their leave.

The pace of the meal is also different in China. In the West, the meal is served quite quickly and conversation continues over a glass of wine or cup of coffee after the meal. The Chinese, on the other hand, allow plenty of time for chatting during the meal itself.

In China, soup is slurped—one drinks rather than eats soup. Its purpose is not to stimulate the appetite but to add a finishing touch to the meal. Soups served at the end of a long menu are only lightly seasoned, to give the taste buds a rest after many hot and spicy, piquant and sweet-and-sour courses.

The type of soup served depends on the time of year—in summer lighter, more delicate soups are preferred, in winter soups are more substantial. In the West, the best-known Chinese soup is hot-and-sour soup, listed on the menu in many Chinese restaurants as "Peking goulash soup", a hearty cold-weather dish.

Soup comes in small porcelain bowls with porcelain spoons. Sometimes it is served with a little rice, although this is not usual on festive occasions.

# San xian soup

*Easy • Special occasion* **San xian tang**

*Serves 4*

*20 g dried Chinese black mushrooms*
*100 g raw prawns*
*100 g skinned, boned chicken breast (about 2 cm thick)*
*2 sprigs coriander*
*¾ litre chicken stock*
*1 tbsp rice wine*
*1 tbsp light soy sauce*
*salt*
*freshly ground white pepper*
*1 tsp sesame oil*

*Preparation time: 30 minutes*

*320 kJ/76 calories per portion*

**1** Soak the mushrooms in warm water for about 10 minutes. Wash and shell the prawns, remove the dark, vein-like intestines *(above)* and pat dry. Cut the prawns in half lengthwise.

**2** Wash the chicken breast, pat dry and cut it into thin slices about 4 cm long. Wash the coriander, shake dry and chop finely.

**3** Bring a saucepan of water to the boil. Add the prawns and chicken slices and blanch in the briskly boiling water for about 1 minute, then remove from the pan and drain through a colander. Remove the black mushrooms from the water, wash, remove the stalks and cut the mushrooms into thin strips.

**4** Bring the chicken stock to the boil in a saucepan. Add the prawns, chicken and mushrooms. Add the rice wine and soy sauce, and season with salt and pepper. Return to the boil and, using a spoon, skim off any scum that forms on the surface. Sprinkle with the coriander and sesame oil, and serve.

**Note:** The expression "San xian" is a very important Chinese culinary term, which means three especially tasty ingredients. The number "three" is not taken too literally; the main aim is to create an imaginative combination for the dish, and the ingredients may include prawns, pork, duck, chicken, fish and dried Chinese mushrooms. In Peking the recipe uses sea cucumber, but dried Chinese black mushrooms are a good substitute.

**Variation:** To make a vegetarian version of this flavoursome soup, replace the prawns and chicken with 100 g bamboo shoots and 2 eggs, and use vegetable instead of chicken stock. Blanch the bamboo shoots in boiling water for about 1 minute. Drain and leave to cool, then cut into thin shreds about 4 cm long. Break the eggs into a bowl, add a little salt, and whisk them. Heat 1 tsp vegetable oil in a wok. Add the beaten egg, gently tilting the pan to spread it in a very thin layer over the base of the wok. Cook over low heat until set. Remove from the pan, leave to cool, then cut into thin strips about 4 cm long. Add the bamboo shoots and shredded omelette to the boiling stock, return to the boil, and season as above.

# Shark's fin soup

**Yu chi tang**

*Takes time • Mild*

*Serves 4*

50 g skinned and boned
chicken breast
10 g dried shark's fin
20 g dried Chinese black
mushrooms
50 g canned bamboo shoot pieces
5 chives
2 tbsp vegetable oil
1 tbsp rice wine
salt
freshly ground white pepper
1 tsp sesame oil

**Preparation time: 1 hour**

**350 kJ/83 calories per portion**

**1** Wash the chicken breast, pat dry and place in a small saucepan. Cover with 65 cl water. Bring to the boil, cover the pan and cook over medium heat for about 15 minutes. Remove the chicken from the pan, reserving the stock, and allow to cool slightly, then cut into shreds about 5 cm long. Meanwhile, soak the shark's fin and mushrooms in warm water for about 10 minutes.

**2** Bring a saucepan of water to the boil and blanch the bamboo shoots in the briskly boiling water for 1 minute, then remove with a slotted spoon, drain, and leave to cool. Cut into strips as thick as a matchstick and about 5 cm long. Wash the chives, shake dry, chop finely, and set aside. Remove the shark's fin and mushrooms from the water. Cut the shark's fin into 5 cm pieces and the mushrooms into thin strips.

**3** Simmer the shark's fin, covered, in the reserved stock over low heat for about 20 minutes, then remove from the pan and drain. Reserve the stock.

**4** Heat the oil in a wok or saucepan over medium heat and briefly stir-fry the mushrooms and bamboo shoots. Add the shark's fin, shredded chicken breast and rice wine, and season with salt and pepper. Pour in the reserved stock, bring to the boil and cook over medium heat for about 3 minutes.

**5** Pour the soup into small bowls, sprinkle with the chives and sesame oil and serve at once.

# Mushroom soup

**Easy • Shandong**  **Dong gu mu xi tang**  *Serves 4*

*10 g dried Chinese black mushrooms*
*5 dried wood ear mushrooms*
*25 g canned bamboo shoot pieces*
*50 g lean pork*
*10 g fresh spinach leaves*
*1 egg*
*salt*
*65 cl vegetable stock*
*freshly ground white pepper*
*1 tsp rice wine*
*1 tsp sesame oil*

*Preparation time: 30 minutes*

*280 kJ/67 calories per portion*

**1** Soak the dried black and wood ear mushrooms separately in warm water for about 10 minutes. Remove from the water and wash, taking care to wash the wood ear mushrooms very thoroughly. Bring a saucepan of water to the boil and blanch the bamboo shoots in the briskly boiling water for about 1 minute, then remove with a slotted spoon, drain and leave to cool.

**2** Wash the meat and pat dry. Trim the spinach and wash thoroughly in a bowl of cold water. Using a sharp knife, cut all the prepared ingredients into shreds about 5 cm long. In a bowl, whisk the egg, adding a little salt.

**3** Bring the stock to the boil in a saucepan. Add the meat and season with salt and pepper. When it comes to the boil, skim any scum from the surface with a spoon. Add the black and wood ear mushrooms, bamboo shoots and spinach.

**4** As soon as the soup comes to the boil again, slowly stir in the beaten egg with a spoon and remove the pan from the heat. Add the rice wine and sprinkle with the sesame oil. Serve at once.

# Hot-and-sour soup

**Easy • Spicy**    **Suan la tang**        *Serves 4*

*50 g pork fillet*
*5 dried wood ear mushrooms*
*10 g cellophane noodles*
*50 g tofu*
*30 g canned bamboo shoot pieces*
*1 spring onion (about 10 cm long)*
*2 sprigs coriander*
*2 tbsp vegetable oil*
*6-8 Sichuan peppercorns*
*1½ tbsp sesame oil for frying*
*8 white peppercorns*
*2 tbsp light soy sauce*
*1 tbsp rice wine*
*1 tbsp cornflour*
*2 eggs*
*2 tbsp dark rice vinegar*

**Preparation time: 40 minutes**

**720 kJ/170 calories per portion**

**1** Wash the pork fillet, pat dry, then place in a saucepan with ¾ litre water. Cover and cook over medium heat for about 15 minutes. Meanwhile, soak the wood ear mushrooms and cellophane noodles separately in warm water for about 10 minutes.

**2** Bring a saucepan of water to the boil and blanch the tofu and bamboo shoots in the briskly boiling water for about 1 minute. Remove from the pan, drain and leave to cool. Cut the tofu into strips about 3 cm long and 1 cm wide. Cut the bamboo shoots into matchstick-sized pieces.

**3** Trim, wash and finely chop the spring onion. Wash the coriander, shake dry and cut both the leaves and stalks into 1 cm pieces.

**4** Pour the vegetable oil into a frying pan and fry the Sichuan peppercorns over low heat for about 1 minute. Strain and reserve the flavoured oil. Remove the cellophane noodles from the water and cut them into pieces about 5 cm long. Remove the wood ear mushrooms from the water, wash thoroughly and cut into strips. Remove the meat from the pan and cut into thin strips. Reserve the pork stock.

**5** Heat the sesame oil in a pan over low heat. Briefly stir-fry the white peppercorns, then remove from the oil with a spoon. Add the spring onions to the oil and stir-fry briefly. Add the reserved stock, increase the heat to medium and bring the stock to the boil.

**6** Add the meat, cellophane noodles, wood ear mushrooms, tofu and bamboo shoots. Season with the light soy sauce and rice wine. Dissolve the cornflour in 4 tbsp water, stir it into the soup and return to the boil.

**7** Whisk the eggs in a bowl and stir them into the boiling soup. Remove from the heat immediately. Add the rice vinegar and sprinkle with the reserved pepper-flavoured oil and the coriander. Serve at once.

**Note:** Tofu, which is made from soya milk, is a popular ingredient in Chinese cookery. It is high in protein and essential fatty acids, and contains vital minerals and vitamins. It is also cholesterol free and low in calories. Tofu is sold in Oriental food stores and health food shops, and is also now available in some supermarkets.

**Variation:** This delicious soup, which many Chinese restaurants call "Peking goulash soup", can be prepared with chicken pieces instead of pork.

# Pickled vegetable soup

*Quick • Spring dish* **Zha cai rou si tang** *Serves 4*

**100 g lean pork**
**80 g zha cai (canned pickled vegetables—see Note)**
**2 sprigs coriander**
**½ litre meat stock**
**1 tbsp rice wine**
**1 tsp sesame oil**

**Preparation time: 20 minutes**

**310 kJ/74 calories per portion**

**1** Wash the pork, pat dry, and cut into thin strips about 5 cm long. Wash the pickled vegetables in cold water and cut into very thin shreds about 5 cm long. Wash the coriander, shake dry and chop finely, then set aside.

**2** Bring the meat stock to the boil in a saucepan, add the shredded pickled vegetables and simmer over low heat for about 5 minutes.

**3** Add the meat strips and continue to cook over medium heat for 1 minute, skimming off any scum that forms on the surface with a slotted spoon. Stir in the rice wine. Sprinkle the chopped coriander and the sesame oil over the top, and serve the soup at once.

**Note:** *Zha cai* (canned pickled vegetables) have a salty and slightly piquant flavour, so there is no need to add salt to the soup. They can be thinly sliced and served as an appetizer. Finely chopped, they blend well with other ingredients, for example fried with pork or steamed with Chinese cabbage. Once opened, any unused *zha cai* should be transferred to a tightly sealed jar. It will keep in the refrigerator for up to two weeks.

**Variation:** For a vegetarian version, omit the pork and add "egg flowers" *(see the recipe below)* to the stock.

# Egg flower soup

*Easy • Summer dish* **Xi hong shi dan hua tang** *Serves 4*

**200 g ripe tomatoes**
**5 chives**
**2 tbsp vegetable oil**
**salt**
**freshly ground white pepper**
**¾ litre vegetable stock**
**2 eggs**
**1 tsp sesame oil**

**Preparation time: 15 minutes**

**430 kJ/100 calories per portion**

**1** Plunge the tomatoes very briefly into boiling water. Rinse and remove the skins. Halve the tomatoes crosswise, remove the seeds and slice thinly. Wash the chives, shake dry, then snip into very small pieces and set aside in a small bowl.

**2** Heat the vegetable oil in a wok over medium heat. Add the sliced tomatoes, season to taste with salt and pepper, and fry briefly. When the oil turns red, add the vegetable stock, turn the heat up high and bring to the boil.

**3** Break the eggs into a bowl and whisk lightly, then trickle them evenly over the soup rather than dropping them in

all at once. Remove the wok from the heat immediately. The strands of egg float on the surface of the soup like flowers as they cook in the soup.

**4** Pour the soup into individual bowls, sprinkle the sesame oil and chopped chives over the top, and serve at once.

**Note:** To thicken this soup, dissolve 2 tbsp cornflour in 2 tbsp water and stir it into the stock before adding the eggs. The thin soup is a very refreshing summer dish, while the thicker version is more suitable for winter.

# NOODLES

There is a widespread belief that the staple food of every Chinese person is rice, but this is only true of southern China. In the north, noodles and other flour-based products take pride of place, and although rice is eaten as well, it is in much smaller quantities than in the south.

Northern Chinese specialities include *mantou* (steamed buns), pancakes, stuffed dumplings and noodles. There are many varieties of *mantou*, which can come plain or with a meat or vegetable filling, or a mixture of both. Stuffed ones are known as *baozi*.

Preparing *baozi* is a time-consuming business, so the problem is solved by a joint effort between family members, neighbours and friends. Working in a cosy atmosphere enlivened by the constant buzz of conversation, one person prepares the dough, another makes the filling, while a third stuffs the dough with the filling.

We know from Marco Polo's travel journals that he was full of praise for the unusual noodles he found in China. From very early in their history, the Chinese recognized the advantages of this simple, starchy, but versatile food. Menus for birthday meals always include very long noodles, a symbol of longevity. One of China's most popular snacks for taking on a journey consists of dried noodles and dried vegetables, reconstituted with boiling water just before you eat them.

# Pork-filled pastry packets

**Guo tie**

*250 g plain flour*
*1 spring onion*
*1 thin slice fresh ginger root*
*150 g minced pork*
*1 tbsp light soy sauce*
*1 tsp rice wine*
*salt*
*6 tbsp vegetable oil*
*1 tsp dark rice vinegar*
*1 tbsp sesame oil per person, as a dip*

*Preparation time: 1 hour (plus 1 hour's resting time)*

*239 kJ/55 calories per packet*

**1** Pour the flour into a bowl. Add about 10 cl warm water, a little at a time, and work to a smooth dough. Wrap it in a damp cloth and leave to rest for about 1 hour. Meanwhile, make the filling. Trim, wash and finely chop the spring onion. Peel and finely chop the ginger.

**2** Mix the minced pork with the spring onion, ginger, soy sauce, rice wine, a little salt and 2 tbsp cold water.

**3** On a lightly floured work surface, shape the dough into a roll measuring about 2.5 cm in diameter.

**4** Divide the dough roll into about 30 pieces. Using a small rolling pin, roll each of the pieces into a circle about 7 cm in diameter *(above)*. The middle of the circle should be a little thicker than the edge. Alternatively, for a slightly quicker, but not so traditional method, roll out the dough on a lightly floured work surface, then use the rim of a glass, about 7 cm in diameter, to cut out the pastry circles.

**5** Place 1 tsp of the filling in the centre of each pastry circle. Fold each circle into a half-moon shape *(above)*, and firmly press the edges together with your fingertips.

**6** Heat the vegetable oil in a frying pan over medium heat. Arrange the pastry packets close together in the pan and fry for about 2 minutes.

**7** Mix the vinegar with about 12.5 cl cold water, pour it over the packets and quickly cover the pan: adding the vinegar makes the pastry pockets nice and crisp on the bottom. Cook the packets for 5 to 7 minutes, until all the water in the pan has evaporated.

**8** Serve the pastry packets with the sesame oil served in little individual bowls as a dip.

**Variation:** Finely chopped Chinese cabbage or Chinese chives can be added to the filling.

# Fried Chinese noodles

**San xian chao mian**

20 g dried Chinese black
mushrooms
100 g raw prawns
100 g skinned and boned
chicken breast
1 egg white
1 tsp cornflour
salt
50 g canned bamboo shoot pieces
200 g medium-thick Chinese
noodles
2½ tbsp light soy sauce
4 tbsp vegetable oil for frying
1 tbsp rice wine
freshly ground white pepper
1 tsp sesame oil (optional)

**Preparation time: 40 minutes**

2,800 kJ/670 calories per portion

**1** Soak the dried mushrooms in warm water for about 10 minutes. Wash and shell the prawns, remove the dark vein-like intestine *(see Step 1, page 110)* and pat dry. Cut the shelled prawns in half lengthwise.

**2** Wash the chicken breast, pat it dry and cut into slices about 4 cm long and 1 cm wide.

**3** Place the halved prawns and sliced chicken in separate bowls, each with half the egg white, ½ tsp cornflour and a little salt. Stir well.

**4** Bring a saucepan of water to the boil and blanch the bamboo shoots in the briskly boiling water for 1 minute, then

remove from the water with a slotted spoon. Drain, leave to cool and cut into strips. Remove the mushrooms from the water, wash and cut into strips.

**5** Preheat the oven to its minimum setting. Meanwhile, bring plenty of water to the boil in a saucepan. Add the noodles, cook for 3 to 5 minutes and drain in a colander. Rinse them under cold running water and drain again. Place in a bowl and mix with 1 tbsp of the soy sauce and a little salt.

**6** Heat a wok over medium heat. Add 2 tbsp of the vegetable oil and heat for about 3 minutes. Add the noodles and

spread them evenly over the base of the pan. Season with 1 tbsp soy sauce and stir thoroughly. Tilt the wok slightly to spread the oil evenly.

**7** Fry the noodles for 2 to 3 minutes, then turn them over and fry for a further 3 minutes, gently stirring with a chopstick from time to time. When the noodles are lightly browned, transfer from the pan to two individual plates and keep warm in the oven.

**8** Add another 1 tbsp oil to the wok and leave over medium heat until hot.

Stir-fry the prawns for about 2 minutes, then remove them from the pan. Heat the remaining oil in the wok and stir-fry the chicken for about 2 minutes.

**9** Add the mushrooms, bamboo shoots and prawns. Season with the rice wine, remaining ½ tbsp soy sauce and salt and pepper. Stir-fry for 1 to 2 minutes, gradually adding 10 cl water. When hot, pour the contents of the wok over the portions of noodles and sprinkle with sesame oil, if liked. Serve at once.

**Variation:** For vegetarians, replace the prawns and chicken with 4 eggs. Break the eggs into a bowl and whisk with a little salt. Heat 4 tbsp vegetable oil in a wok over medium heat. Add the beaten eggs, cook until set, then cut into small pieces. Fry briefly with the mushrooms and bamboo shoots.

Instead of Chinese noodles, you can use spaghetti, if preferred.

# Stuffed dumplings

*Takes time • Many regions*

**Shao mai**

*Makes 20*

200 g plain flour
1 spring onion
200 g minced pork
1 egg white
1 tbsp rice wine
½ tsp sugar
salt
20 frozen peas

**Preparation time: 45 minutes
(plus 20 minutes' standing time)**

**230 kJ/55 calories per dumpling**

**1** In a bowl, mix the flour with about 10 cl cold water and knead to a smooth dough. Cover with a damp cloth and leave to stand for about 20 minutes.

**2** Meanwhile, trim, wash and finely chop the spring onion. Mix the minced meat with the spring onion, egg white, rice wine, sugar and a little salt, and divide into 20 portions.

**3** Knead the dough again, then shape into a roll about 2 cm in diameter and cut into 20 equal pieces. Knead each piece and then roll into a circle about 6 cm in diameter.

**4** Hold a pastry circle flat in one hand. Place a portion of meat filling on top

and wrap the dough around it, so that the dumpling is open at the top and looks like a little bag. Place a frozen pea at the opening of each dumpling.

**5** Line a bamboo steamer with a damp cloth. Arrange the dumplings in the steamer about 1 cm apart and replace the lid. Bring about ½ litre water to the boil in a wok or pan into which the steamer will fit. Steam the dumplings for about 10 minutes. (*See Note, page 50*, if you do not have a bamboo steamer.)

# Noodles with meat sauce

*Quick • Peking*

**Zha jiang mian**

*Serves 2*

20 g dried Chinese black
mushrooms
40 g canned bamboo shoot pieces
1 hazelnut-sized piece fresh
ginger root
1 leek (about 150 g)
200 g wide Chinese noodles
2 tbsp vegetable oil
125 g minced pork
100 g yellow bean paste
1 tsp rice wine
5 cl meat stock
1 tsp sesame oil

**Preparation time: 30 minutes**

**1,900 kJ/450 calories per portion**

**1** Soak the mushrooms in warm water for about 10 minutes. Meanwhile, bring a saucepan of water to the boil. Blanch the bamboo shoots in the briskly boiling water for about 1 minute. Drain, leave to cool, then chop the bamboo shoots into very small dice (smaller than a pea). Peel the ginger. Trim and wash the leek. Finely chop the ginger and leek. Remove the mushrooms from the water and dice finely.

**2** Bring a large saucepan of water to the boil and add the noodles and cook for about 10 minutes. Meanwhile, heat the vegetable oil in a frying pan or wok over medium heat. Briefly stir-fry the ginger and leek, then add the meat,

diced bamboo shoots and mushrooms, and stir-fry for 1 minute. Add the bean paste and bring briefly to the boil.

**3** Stir in the rice wine and cook for a further 1 minute, stirring constantly. When the pork begins to disintegrate in the hot sauce, add the meat stock and stir thoroughly.

**4** Drain the noodles and transfer to a shallow serving bowl. Pour the meat sauce over them. Sprinkle with the sesame oil and serve at once.

**Variation:** For a vegetarian dish, omit the minced pork and use about 200 g very finely diced aubergine instead.

# Spring rolls
## San si chun juan

**5 dried Chinese black mushrooms**
**150 g lean pork**
**salt**
**freshly ground black pepper**
**2 tbsp rice wine**
**2 tbsp cornflour**
**1 medium-sized Chinese cabbage**
**(about 300 g)**
**1½ tbsp sesame oil**
**12 thawed frozen spring roll**
**wrappers (about 20 cm square)**
**1 egg**
**1 litre vegetable oil**

**Preparation time: 1 hour**
**20 minutes**

**530 kJ/150 calories per roll**

**1** Soak the mushrooms in warm water for about 10 minutes. Meanwhile, cut the meat into strips about 5 mm thick and 5 cm long. Place the strips in a bowl and season with salt and pepper. Stir in the rice wine and 1 tbsp of the cornflour, and leave to marinate for about 10 minutes. Wash the Chinese cabbage, cut in half lengthwise, then cut crosswise into shreds 5 mm wide. Wash, drain and shred the mushrooms.

**2** Heat the sesame oil in a wok and stir-fry the meat over high heat for about 2 minutes, then remove from the pan. Add the cabbage and mushrooms to the wok. Stir-fry over medium heat for 5 to 10 minutes, then return the meat and season with salt and pepper.

**3** Dissolve the remaining cornflour in a little cold water and stir it into the pan to bind the meat and vegetable mixture. Remove all the ingredients from the pan and leave to cool.

**4** Separate the thawed spring roll wrappers. Lay one wrapper flat on the work surface. Place 2 tbsp of the filling neatly at one end of the wrapper, leaving space around the edges. Whisk the egg. Brush the edges with beaten egg, fold both sides inwards, then roll up, sealing with beaten egg. Repeat the process with all the spring rolls.

**5** Heat the vegetable oil in a wok or pan over high heat until small bubbles rise from a wooden chopstick dipped in the hot fat. Deep-fry the spring rolls for about 5 minutes, until golden-brown. Remove from the pan and serve.

# Vegetable dumplings

**Su cai bao zi**

**250 g plain flour**
**3½ g dried yeast**
**50 g cellophane noodles**
**5 dried tiger lily buds**
**5 dried Chinese black mushrooms**
**1 medium-sized Chinese cabbage**
**(about 300 g)**
**salt**
**3 tbsp sesame oil**
**freshly ground black pepper**

**Preparation time: 1½ hours**

**490 kJ/120 calories per dumpling**

**1** Place the flour in a bowl. In another bowl, dissolve the yeast in a generous 12.5 cl lukewarm water, then add it to the flour. Knead the dough thoroughly until it is smooth and elastic and does not stick to your fingers. Cover it with a damp cloth and leave to rise in a warm place for about 20 minutes.

**2** Meanwhile, soak the noodles, tiger lily buds and mushrooms in separate, bowls of warm water for 20 minutes. Meanwhile, wash the Chinese cabbage and chop very finely. Sprinkle it lightly with salt, leave for 10 minutes, then squeeze out the moisture. Drain the noodles, mushrooms and tiger lily buds, wash, drain and chop finely, then stir them into the cabbage with the sesame oil. Season with salt and pepper.

**3** Knead the dough a second time. On a floured work surface, shape the dough into a roll about 2 cm in diameter, and cut it into 12 equal-sized pieces.

**4** Roll out each piece to a circle about 8 cm in diameter, with the middle thicker than the edge. Take each circle in one hand, spread a portion of filling in the middle and, starting from one side, pull the edge of the pastry upwards and make a pleat. Continue to make pleats all the way round—always pulling the dough up a little to keep the thickness even—until it completely covers the filling. Finally, lightly twist the pleated edges to form a little closed pouch. *(See Steps 3 and 4, page 136.)*

**5** Pour water into a wok to a level of 3 to 4 cm and bring to the boil. Line a bamboo steamer with a damp cloth. Arrange the dumplings in the steamer at least 2 cm apart. Replace the lid on the steamer and carefully stand it over the wok. Steam the dumplings over high heat for about 20 minutes. *(See Note, page 50, if you do not have a bamboo steamer.)*

# DESSERTS AND SWEETMEATS

If you try to order a dessert at the end of a lengthy restaurant meal in northern China, you will often be disappointed. Desserts in the true sense of the word are unknown in Chinese cuisine.

Instead of desserts, there is an amazing range of sweetmeats to eat "between times". They might be served as an afternoon snack, or offered to visitors as a means of persuading them to stay for dinner.

In the same way as Westerners celebrate a birthday with a cake, there are special sweetmeats for certain high days and holidays. Sweet dishes are also an essential part of festive meals like wedding banquets. They are traditionally served between courses.

Usually, sweetmeats are made with bean paste, lotus seeds, glutinous rice or fruit. Any of the sweetmeats in this chapter could be served as a sweet and refreshing dessert, to round off a home-cooked Chinese meal.

# Cornmeal hats

*Easy • Very sweet* **Xiao wo tou** *Makes 30 cakes*

*160 g finely ground cornmeal*
*50 g soya flour*
*75 to 100 g sugar (according to taste)*

*Preparation time: 30 minutes*

*150 kJ/36 calories per cake*

**1** Mix together the cornmeal, soya flour and sugar in a bowl. Add about 10 cl lukewarm water and knead for 6 to 7 minutes to make a smooth, elastic dough that does not stick to your fingers.

**2** Shape the dough into a long roll about 2 cm in diameter, then cut the roll into 30 equal-sized pieces.

**3** Have a bowl of cold water ready. Holding a piece of dough in one hand, dip the other hand briefly in the water. Knead the dough once again and shape into a ball. Dip your index finger in the cold water, then make a round hollow in the middle of the ball *(above)*.

**4** Carefully form the ball into a little pointed hat shape, then repeat the same process with all the dough balls to make 30 little cakes *(above)*.

**5** Line a bamboo steamer with a damp cloth and arrange the shaped cakes in the steamer about 1 cm apart, then replace the lid. Bring ½ litre water to the boil in a saucepan, then stand the steamer over the saucepan and steam the little cakes over high heat for about 10 minutes. *(See Note, page 50, if you do not have a bamboo steamer.)*

**6** Remove the cooked cakes from the steamer and serve at once.

**Note:** The saying "Hunger is the best cook" holds good even for royalty. When the Empress Dowager Ci Xi fled Peking to escape the Boxer uprising in 1900, she was driven by hunger to eat cornmeal rolls offered to her by a peasant. She found them so tasty that, on her return to the capital, her cooks were ordered to make similar rolls. The result was, of course, much more refined than the peasant's cornmeal offering, but there is no truth in the story that Ci Xi's cooks used chestnut flour to make these cornmeal hats.

# Toffee apples

**Easy • Peking**

## Ba si ping guo

*Serves 4*

*1 tbsp black sesame seeds*
*400 g tart, crisp apples (for example, Granny Smiths)*
*50 g cornflour*
*2 egg whites*
*½ litre vegetable oil for deep-frying*
*2 tbsp sesame oil*
*100 g sugar*

*Preparation time: 25 minutes*

*1400 kJ/330 calories per portion*

**1** Stir-fry the sesame seeds in a small pan without fat over low heat for about 3 minutes. Peel and core the apples, then cut into diamond-shaped pieces about 4 cm long and 2 cm wide.

**2** Place the cornflour and egg whites in a bowl and mix thoroughly. Coat the apple pieces in the batter.

**3** Heat the vegetable oil in a wok or pan over high heat, until small bubbles rise from a wooden chopstick dipped in the hot fat. Deep-fry the apples for about 3 minutes, until golden. Using a slotted spoon, remove the apple pieces from the fat and drain off the fat. Pour off the oil from the wok.

**4** Pour the sesame oil into the wok, followed by the sugar. Stir-fry over low heat until the sugar melts. You may have to take the wok off the heat from time to time, to prevent burning.

**5** When the sugar begins to bubble, add the apples and toss briefly in the hot toffee. Transfer the apples to a plate and sprinkle with the toasted sesame seeds.

**6** Provide each person with a small bowl of cold water. The toffee apple pieces should be dipped in the water before eating. The coating becomes nice and crisp, and forms sugary threads.

**Drink:** Toffee apples are good with a glass of port.

# Almond pudding

*Simple • Refreshing*  **Xing ren dou fu**                                    *Serves 4*

**70 g shelled almonds**
**6 g gelatine (3½ leaves)**
**4 cl milk**
**80 g sugar**
**40 g canned mandarin oranges**

**Preparation time: 20 minutes**
**(plus 2 hours´ chilling time)**

**840 kJ/200 calories per portion**

**1** Soak the almonds in enough warm water to cover, for about 15 minutes. Meanwhile, soak the gelatine in cold water for about 10 minutes and then squeeze thoroughly. Remove the almonds from the water and peel them. Place the peeled almonds in a food processor with 20 cl water and grind to a milky liquid.

**2** Strain the almond liquid through a coffee filter into a saucepan. Add the milk and bring to the boil. Stir in the gelatine and continue to stir until it has dissolved. Pour the mixture into a round dish, 25 to 30 cm in diameter and about 2 cm deep, and allow the pudding to cool.

**3** Rinse the saucepan. Add 10 cl water and stir in the sugar. Bring the water to the boil. Stir over low heat until the sugar has dissolved, then pour into a bowl and leave to cool.

**4** Chill the almond pudding and sugar water in the refrigerator for 2 hours.

**5** When you are ready to serve, cut the pudding into diamond-shaped pieces and divide between individual bowls. Add the mandarin oranges. Pour the sugar water over the top and serve.

**Note:** This is an ideal dessert with which to conclude a sumptuous meal, especially in hot weather. Other fruit, such as pineapple, can be used instead of mandarins.

**Variation:** Although almond essence is unknown in China, you can use 6 to 8 drops of essence instead of almonds, if time is short. Prepare the gelatine. Bring the milk and 20 cl water to the boil and stir in the gelatine. Stir the almond essence into the mixture, pour into the round dish and continue as described above.

# Fried honey bananas

*Easy • Many regions* **Dan bai xiang jiao jia xian** *Serves 4*

*1 tbsp black sesame seeds*
*4 bananas*
*100 g Dou sha (sweet bean paste—see Note, page 136)*
*30 g flour*
*20 to 25 g cornflour*
*2 egg whites*
*1 litre vegetable oil for deep-frying*
*5 tbsp clear honey*

*Preparation time: 30 minutes*

*1,700 kJ/400 calories per portion*

**1** Preheat the oven to its minimum setting. Stir-fry the sesame seeds in a small pan without fat over low heat for about 3 minutes, then remove from the pan and set aside.

**2** Peel the bananas and cut them in half crosswise, then cut lengthwise into slices 1 cm thick. Spread half the banana slices with bean paste, then lay the remaining halves on top to make "sandwiches". Coat the bananas in the flour. In a shallow bowl, mix the cornflour with the egg whites. Put a serving plate to warm in the oven.

**3** Heat the oil in a wok or pan. Dip the banana sandwiches in the cornflour batter, drain off any excess batter then deep-fry them, one at a time, in the oil for 1 to 2 minutes, until golden. Drain briefly and arrange on the warm plate.

**4** Drizzle the honey over the bananas, and sprinkle with the sesame seeds. Serve the bananas while still warm.

**Note:** The bananas look very pretty arranged in a star shape around a slice of candied orange.

# Candied potato balls

*Easy • Shandong* **Ba si jin zao** *Serves 4 (Makes 20)*

*300 g floury potatoes*
*50 g flour*
*150 g candied fruit (for example, cherries, orange and lemon peel)*
*½ litre vegetable oil for deep-frying*
*2 to 3 tbsp sesame oil*
*100 g sugar*

*Preparation time: 45 minutes*

*1,900 kJ/450 calories per portion*

**1** Wash and peel the potatoes. Cook in boiling water, covered, for 15 to 20 minutes, then drain and mash. Add the flour, knead thoroughly and shape into a roll about 4 cm in diameter. Divide the potato dough into 20 pieces. With the palm of your hand, press them into long, flat shapes.

**2** Finely chop the candied fruit and divide it into 20 portions. Place one portion of fruit on each potato dough shape and carefully shape the dough around the filling to form a ball. Press together any splits in the dough.

**3** Heat the vegetable oil in a wok or pan over high heat until small bubbles rise from a wooden chopstick dipped in the hot fat. Deep-fry the potato balls for about 3 minutes, until they are golden. Remove the potato balls from the pan and drain off the fat. Pour off the oil from the wok.

**4** Pour the sesame oil into the wok, followed by the sugar. Stir over low heat until the sugar melts. You may have to take the wok off the heat from time to time while the sugar is melting to prevent it burning.

**5** When the sugar begins to bubble, briefly toss the potato balls, one by one, in the toffee, then arrange them on a serving dish.

**6** Provide each person with a small bowl of cold water. The potato balls should be dipped in the water before eating. The coating becomes nice and crisp, and forms sugary threads.

# Bean paste dumplings

**Dou sha bao**

*Takes time • Many regions*

*Makes 20*

**500 g plain flour**
**20 g fresh yeast**
**400 g Dou sha (sweet bean paste—see Note)**

**Preparation time: 1½ hours (plus 30 minutes' rising time)**

**550 kJ/130 calories per dumpling**

**1** Place the flour in a bowl. Dissolve the yeast in ¼ litre lukewarm water and add to the flour. Knead thoroughly then cover with a slightly damp cloth and leave to rise in a warm place for about 30 minutes.

**2** Knead the dough thoroughly again. On a lightly floured surface, shape the dough into a roll, about 2.5 cm in diameter, and cut it into 20 pieces. Roll out each piece to a round about 10 cm in diameter. The middle of each round should be thicker than the edges.

**3** Spread 1 tbsp of the sweet bean paste over the middle of each pastry round. Starting from one side, pull the edge of the pastry upwards and make a pleat *(above)*.

**4** Continue to make pleats all the way round until the dough completely covers the filling. Twist the pleated edges to form a closed pouch *(above)*.

**5** Bring some water to the boil in a saucepan. Line a bamboo steamer with a damp cloth, arrange the first batch of dumplings about 2 to 3 cm apart in the steamer and replace the lid.

**6** Stand the steamer over the pan and steam the dumplings over high heat for about 10 to 12 minutes. *(See Note, page 50,* if you do not have a bamboo steamer.) Cover the cooked dumplings and keep warm while cooking the remaining batches. Serve them hot or warm.

**Note:** *Dou sha* (sweet bean paste) is made from red beans and sugar (or crystallized sugar). The beans are cooked for 1 to 2 hours, until very soft, and then pressed through a sieve. The paste is mainly used to fill cakes and sweetmeats. Canned sweet bean paste is sold in Oriental food stores.

**Variation:** Instead of the sweet bean paste, briefly toast 300 g black sesame seeds, crush them using a pestle and mortar, then mix with 100 g sugar. Poppy seed paste makes another tasty filling for dumplings.

# Suggested Menus

A meal in China is very much a social occasion. Generally, a large number of people gather to eat together—whether family sharing a meal at home, or a group of friends or business associates meeting at a restaurant—so it is possible to have a variety of dishes. Food is served in large serving dishes which are placed in the middle of the table for everyone to help themselves from. The quantities indicated in most of the recipes in this book are sufficient for a serving dish for two or four people.

If creating your own menu, here are a few hints:
• The colours of each dish should harmonize, as should colours of the entire meal.
• Avoid too many dishes with a similar taste—provide a variety of flavours.
• Lay the table Chinese-style, with a small porcelain plate, a bowl and chopsticks for each guest. According to Chinese etiquette, the porcelain bowl should be held in one hand and not left standing on the table.
• Even if all you have is a chicken and a few ingredients, divide up the chicken and prepare each portion with different and contrasting ingredients.
• Try following the authentic Chinese custom of serving a light soup at the end of the meal.

Some of the menus below suggest fresh fruit or ice cream for dessert. As there is no recipe in the book for these, they are marked with an asterisk.

### Menus to prepare in advance

| | |
|---|---:|
| Spicy bamboo shoots | 34 |
| Sweet-and-sour pork | 73 |
| Fried celery | 104 |
| Egg flower soup | 117 |
| Fresh fruit * | — |
| | |
| Prawns with cabbage | 30 |
| Chicken with black beans | 58 |
| Beans with garlic | 101 |
| Pickled vegetable soup | 117 |
| Vanilla ice cream * | — |
| | |
| Chicken with mustard | 30 |
| Prawns with green pepper | 82 |
| Bean sprouts with ginger | 106 |
| Mushroom soup | 113 |
| Fried honey bananas | 135 |

### Simple menu for 2 to 4

| | |
|---|---:|
| Spicy bamboo shoots | 34 |
| Bean sprouts with ginger | 106 |
| Pork fillet with coriander | 75 |
| Egg flower soup | 117 |

### Menus for 4

| | |
|---|---:|
| Tofu with leek | 101 |
| Sweet-and-sour pork | 73 |
| Prawns with green pepper | 82 |
| Hot-and-sour soup | 114 |
| Toffee apples | 132 |
| | |
| Fried celery | 104 |
| Fried pork | 74 |
| Trout in vinegar sauce | 87 |
| Mushroom soup | 113 |
| Candied potato balls | 135 |
| | |
| Hot Chinese cabbage | 38 |
| Chicken with mushrooms | 54 |
| Bean sprouts with ginger | 106 |
| Pickled vegetable soup | 117 |
| Toffee apples | 132 |
| | |
| Hot Chinese cabbage | 38 |
| Little tofu boxes | 94 |
| Pork with almonds | 73 |
| Hot-and-sour soup | 114 |
| Almond pudding | 133 |

### Menu for 6

| | |
|---|---:|
| Hot Chinese cabbage | 38 |
| Glazed walnuts | 35 |
| Braised aubergines | 102 |
| Chicken with black beans | 58 |
| Trout in vinegar sauce | 87 |
| San xian soup | 110 |
| Toffee apples | 132 |

### Menu for 8

| | |
|---|---:|
| Chicken with noodles | 33 |
| Prawns with cabbage | 30 |
| Spicy mushrooms | 36 |
| Beans with garlic | 101 |
| Fried fillet of beef | 70 |
| Chicken with pineapple | 60 |
| Sizzling rice with prawns | 80 |
| Mushroom soup | 113 |

## Menu for 8 to 10

| | |
|---|---|
| Beef with five spices | 29 |
| Chicken with mustard | 30 |
| Hot Chinese cabbage | 38 |
| Marbled eggs | 36 |
| Crispy fried duck | 49 |
| Shandong chicken | 50 |
| Prawns with green pepper | 82 |
| Beans with garlic | 101 |
| Pork-filled pastry packets | 120 |
| Cornmeal hats | 130 |
| Stuffed dumplings | 124 |
| Almond pudding | 133 |

## Vegetarian menu for 2

| | |
|---|---|
| Little tofu boxes | 94 |
| Egg flower soup | 117 |
| Toffee apples | 132 |

## Vegetarian menu for 4

| | |
|---|---|
| Hot Chinese cabbage | 38 |
| Braised aubergines | 102 |
| Tofu with leek | 101 |
| Beans with garlic | 101 |
| Egg flower soup | 117 |
| Fried honey bananas | 135 |

## Vegetarian menu for 8

| | |
|---|---|
| Spicy bamboo shoots | 34 |
| Marbled eggs | 36 |
| Spicy mushrooms | 36 |
| Eggs with mushrooms | 96 |
| Little tofu boxes | 94 |
| Silver ears with vegetables | 103 |
| Braised aubergines | 102 |
| Egg flower soup | 117 |

## Spring menu

| | |
|---|---|
| Sweet-and-sour cucumber | 101 |
| Duck with *fu zhu* | 46 |
| Sizzling rice with prawns | 80 |
| Bean sprouts with ginger | 106 |
| San xian soup | 110 |
| Stuffed dumplings | 124 |

## Summer menu

| | |
|---|---|
| Chicken with noodles | 33 |
| Barbecued lamb | 66 |
| Spicy chicken wings | 53 |
| Cornmeal hats | 130 |
| Almond pudding | 133 |

## Autumn menu

| | |
|---|---|
| Glazed walnuts | 35 |
| Chicken with chestnuts | 52 |
| Sweet-and-sour carp | 85 |
| Beans with garlic | 101 |
| Shark's fin soup | 112 |
| Honeydew melon * | – |

## Winter menu

| | |
|---|---|
| Hot Chinese cabbage | 38 |
| Lamb with leeks | 67 |
| Braised belly of pork | 71 |
| Tofu hotpot | 98 |
| Hot-and-sour soup | 114 |
| Candied potato balls | 135 |

## Spring Festival menu

| | |
|---|---|
| Chicken with noodles | 33 |
| Spicy bamboo shoots | 34 |
| Peking duck | 42 |
| Silver ears with vegetables | 103 |
| San xian soup | 110 |
| Pork-filled pastry packets | 120 |
| Toffee apples | 132 |

## Moon Festival menu

| | |
|---|---|
| Beef with five spices | 29 |
| Prawns with cabbage | 30 |
| Duck parcels | 45 |
| Braised belly of pork | 71 |
| Squid rolls | 90 |
| Beans with garlic | 101 |
| Sweet-and-sour cucumber | 101 |
| San xian soup | 110 |
| Fried honey bananas | 135 |

# Glossary

*This glossary is intended as a brief guide to some less familiar cookery terms and ingredients, including words and items found on Chinese menus.*

**Bamboo shoots:** the shoots of tropical bamboo. Sold canned in the West, the best-quality bamboo shoots are known as winter bamboo. Ordinary bamboo is less tender. They should be drained and thoroughly rinsed before use. Stored in water in the refrigerator, they will keep for up to a week.

**Bamboo steamer:** an important Chinese cooking utensil, a round basket with a base and lid of woven bamboo, placed over a wok for steaming. Various sizes of bamboo steamers can be bought in specialist oriental shops.

**Bean paste:** flavouring agent in Chinese cuisine. *See also* Yellow bean paste, Hot bean paste and Red bean paste.

**Bean sprouts:** are rich in protein and vitamins. There are two types: mung bean sprouts (*lu dou ya*) and soya bean sprouts (*huang dou ya*). northern Chinese cooks use mostly mung bean sprouts, served raw or briefly fried. *See also page 106.*

**Black mushrooms:** Also known as Shiitake mushrooms. *See box, page 54.*

**Cellophane noodles:** also called bean thread noodles, these are noodles made from mung bean starch, or sometimes from soya bean starch. *See also page 33.*

**Chao:** translates as stir-frying, one of the most important Chinese culinary techniques. Ingredients are constantly stirred in the wok as they cook, so that they quickly become tender but remain firm to the bite.

**Chili peppers:** a variety of hot or mild peppers, mostly used dried in Chinese cookery. They contain volatile oils that can irritate the skin and cause eyes to burn, so handle with caution and wash hands immediately after use.

**Chili sauce:** hot, bright red or orange sauce made from chili peppers, vinegar and salt. Comes in various strengths, and is used mainly as a dipping sauce. Do not confuse with **Chili bean sauce**, made from beans and chilies, which is thicker and used mainly in cooking.

**Chinese chives:** also called garlic chives. Herbs similar to, but stronger than, Western chives, and with a garlic flavour. Not always easy to find.

**Chinese cabbage:** also called Chinese leaves, perhaps northern China's most important vegetable. It is highly versatile and can successfully be pickled, steamed or fried, or combined with any number of other ingredients. *See also page 39.*

**Chopsticks:** Chinese eating utensils made from a wide variety of materials, such as wood, bamboo, plastic, steel, silver or ivory. Many more modest restaurants provide "hygienic" chopsticks. These are pairs of bamboo chopsticks still attached to each other—as a guarantee that they have not been used before—which have to be broken apart before use. Chinese chopsticks are longer and less pointed than those from Japan or Korea.

**Cooking methods:** special methods have been developed in northern China, some borrowed from Mongolian cuisine. The most typical are *bao, shuan* and *kao*. **Bao** means cooking ingredients for a very short time over an extremely high heat, so that they still have plenty of bite. There are five categories of *bao: youbao*, ingredients are marinated in a cornflour paste or similar solution, briefly blanched, then fried in hot oil; *yanbao*, similar to *youbao* but replacing the cornflour with plenty of coriander (squid rolls, *see page 90*, or pork fillet with coriander, *page 75*); *congbao*, like *yanbao* but with leek and garlic instead of coriander (lamb with leeks, *see page 67*); *jiangbao*, meat is marinated in yellow soya bean paste and spices, then fried in hot oil (chicken breast with walnuts, *see page 49*); *shuibao*, ingredients are cooked in boiling water. **Shuan** means finely

shredded ingredients cooked in stock (firepot, *see page 62*). **Kao** means grilling and is an excellent way of preparing lamb (skewered lamb, *see page 66*).

**Coriander:** pungent, peppery herb, used in China for thousands of years. Whole sprigs may be stir-fried with other ingredients or it may be finely chopped and sprinkled over the finished dish.

**"Eight delicacies":** this expression does not mean any specific ingredients, but can be applied to the kind of delicacies not used every day, such as prawns, bamboo shoots, shiitake mushrooms, lotus seeds or ginkgo nuts.

**Fermented black beans:** fermented soya beans preserved with salt and spices, a popular seasoning for fish, meat and poultry. *See also page 59.*

**Firepot:** widely used in northern China for cooking food at the table.

**Five-spice powder:** a pungent, finely ground blend of Sichuan pepper, fennel seeds, star anise, cloves and cinnamon.

**Fu zhu:** dried soya bean curd, available in thin, flat sheets or thinly rolled sticks from specialist Oriental shops. *See also page 47.*

**Garlic:** an ingredient used for thousands of years. With spring onions and leek, garlic is very popular as a pungent seasoning. It can also be pickled in vinegar and sugar. In the province of Shandong, they even like to eat it raw.

**Ginger:** along with spring onion, garlic and leek, one of the main seasoning ingredients in northern Chinese cookery and an absolute must for fish dishes. Always try to use fresh rather than ground ginger.

**Ginkgo nut:** small, shiny, sweet nut used in both sweet and savoury dishes.

**Hoisin sauce:** a thick sweet and spicy sauce used as a dip. It is made from soya beans, wheat flour, vinegar, sugar, salt, garlic, sesame seeds and red rice, giving colour to food. *Hoisin* is a Cantonese word now widely adopted in Europe.

**Hot bean paste** *(la dou ban jiang):* made from yellow and black beans, garlic and chilies.

**La mian:** special technique for producing noodles. Dough made from wheat flour and water is repeatedly kneaded, tossed, beaten and spun to make thin noodles.

**Lotus seeds:** oval seeds of the lotus, a plant related to the water lily, used for decoration and in desserts and sweet pastes. Available canned or dried; if using dried seeds, soak for 8 hours before use, changing the water frequently, to get rid of the bitter taste.

**Mantou:** there is a huge variety of these steamed yeast dough buns. They can be filled with meat, vegetables or a mixture of both, and served at any time. *Mantou* are a popular packed meal for travellers.

**Marinating:** before cooking, ingredients are mixed with seasoning, such as rice wine, soy sauce or pepper, and left to stand so that they take on either flavour or colour.

**Oil:** for Chinese cookery it is best to use soya or groundnut oil. Sunflower oil will do, but never use olive oil. Its distinctive flavour is completely unsuitable for Chinese dishes. In China, pork dripping is often used for cooking to add flavour.

**Pak choi:** Cantonese name for a fresh green vegetable related to Chinese cabbage and Swiss chard. It has thick, white stalks and dark green leaves. Its characteristic flavour blends especially well with pork.

**Pancakes:** among the Chinese names for pancakes are *jian bing* and *lao bing*. Made from wheat flour and water, or from yeast dough, they are very popular in northern China. In Shandong, pancakes wrapped around leeks are a particular favourite.

**Pickled duck eggs:** a popular appetizer, sometimes known by the Chinese name, *song hua dan.*

**Red bean paste** *(hong don sha):* very sweet and used mainly in desserts, is made from red beans and sugar. Bean pastes are available in jars or cans. If refrigerated after opening, they will keep for months.

**Red dates:** small, red, not-too-sweet fruit, used mainly for desserts and sweetmeats. They are also important as a remedy in traditional Chinese medicine.

**Rice vinegar:** condiment available in three varieties: white vinegar is clear and mild; red is sweet and spicy; black has more body. The dark vinegar, which is milder than European vinegar, is the most frequently used.

**Rice wine:** also known as *Shaoxing* after a village in Zhejiang province, famous for its production. The amber-coloured wine is made from rice. It can be warmed, or drunk at room temperature, and is widely used to add flavour to Chinese dishes. Medium-dry sherry is a good substitute.

**San xian:** term used to indicate that a dish includes three particularly delicious ingredients, for example, prawns, chicken and shiitake mushrooms. They do not always have to be the same three.

**Sesame oil:** oil produced from roasted sesame seeds that has a nutty, smoky aroma; used mainly as a seasoning.

**Sesame paste:** thick paste made from toasted white sesame seeds, similar to Middle Eastern tahini, sold in jars.

**Sesame seeds:** tiny black or white seeds from the sesame plant used for oil, paste and sweet dishes and pastries.

**Shiitake mushrooms:** *see box, page 54*

**Shark's fin:** in China there are various types of shark's fin. As a rule, the dried cartilage of the fin is used. This has to be soaked overnight before cooking. In Chinese restaurants in Europe, shark's fin is found only as a soup ingredient.

**Sichuan peppercorns:** *hua jiao* in Chinese, also called Szechwan peppercorns. The reddish-brown dried berries are an important seasoning in northern Chinese specialities.

**Soy sauce:** an essential seasoning in Chinese cuisine, made from fermented soya beans, salt, wheat and yeast. Although available as light or dark soy sauce, there is hardly any difference in the colour of the two varieties. Light soy sauce retains the original colour of the ingredients, while the darker sort gives food a very intense flavour. Chili peppers are added to hot soy sauce.

**Soya milk:** produced by grinding and filtering soaked and heated soya beans.

**Spring onions:** a basic ingredient in northern Chinese cuisine, usually finely chopped and mixed with ginger.

**Spring rolls:** thin pastry wrappers filled with meat and/or vegetables and deep-fried. A sweet version of spring rolls has a filling of sweet bean paste. They are so called because they are prepared for the Spring Festival, which begins with the Chinese New Year. Spring roll wrappers are tricky to make but are available frozen from Oriental food stores.

**Star anise:** the dried, star-shaped fruit of a southern Chinese tree; used in cooking for its liquorice flavour.

**Starch:** the most common forms of starch used in north Chinese cuisine are cornflour or potato starch. The starch is mixed with egg white and/or water, sometimes with the addition of a dash of rice wine, to create thick or runny batter. Ingredients are then dipped in the batter and fried. Starch is also dissolved in water and stirred into sauces to bind them and to ensure that the ingredients are evenly coated.

**Steaming:** a popular cooking method in northern China. Food is placed in a bamboo steamer over a wok filled with boiling water and cooked over the hot steam. To cook different ingredients at the same time, several steamers can be stacked one on top of another. Many woks have a metal steamer attachment on which you can stand plates or bowls. If necessary, you can place an upturned cup in a large pan, and add enough water to reach 3 to 4 cm up the side of the cup. Stand a plate containing the ingredients on top of the cup, cover and steam.

**Stuffed dumplings:** *jiaozi* in Chinese, a typical side dish in northern China and extremely popular with Europeans.

**Tiger lily buds:** also called golden needles, these dried flower buds are a very popular ingredient in vegetarian dishes. *See also page 97.*

**Tofu:** the Japanese pronunciation of the Chinese words *dou fu* has been adopted in the West. The dense, mild soya bean product is also called bean curd. Available in a soft, junket-like variety used in soups, or in firm cakes used for stir-frying, braising or poaching. Sold fresh or vaccuum-packed, tofu will keep refrigerated in water for up to 5 days. Drain well before using.

**Wok:** classic Chinese cooking pan that, because of its rounded shape, ensures even heat when stir-frying. In the past, when woks were used over an open fire, they all had a dome-shaped base. Now, however, you can also buy flat-bottomed woks for cooking on electric hotplates, and table woks, which, like a fondue, stand in the centre of the table and are heated electrically or over a spirit lamp. The wok should be heated first, then brushed with a little cold oil and re-heated. Only then should you add the rest of the oil and begin cooking, so avoiding the cornflour coating of the ingredients sticking to the pan. A heavy frying pan is a suitable alternative.

**Wood ear mushrooms:** also called cloud ear mushrooms, tree ears and tree fungi. Black wood ears are mild and aromatic and combine well with many different ingredients. The white *yin er* or silver ear mushrooms are highly nutritious and regarded as a delicacy. Available dried.

**Yellow bean paste** *(tian mian jiang):* used for Peking duck and other meat dishes, it is a thick salty paste made from yellow beans, flour and salt.

**Zha cai:** pickled vegetables, usually white radish, with salt, chili and other seasonings.

## Recipe Index

### CONVERSION CHART

*These figures are not exact equivalents, but have been rounded up or down slightly to make measuring easier.*

| Weight Equivalents | | Volume Equivalents | |
|---|---|---|---|
| Metric | Imperial | Metric | Imperial |
| 15 g | ½ oz | 8 cl | 3 fl oz |
| 30 g | 1 oz | 12.5 cl | 4 fl oz |
| 60 g | 2 oz | 15 cl | ¼ pint |
| 90 g | 3 oz | 17.5 cl | 6 fl oz |
| 125 g | ¼ lb | 25 cl | 8 fl oz |
| 150 g | 5 oz | 30 cl | ½ pint |
| 200 g | 7 oz | 35 cl | 12 fl oz |
| 250 g | ½ lb | 45 cl | ¾ pint |
| 350 g | ¾ lb | 50 cl | 16 fl oz |
| 500 g | 1 lb | 60 cl | 1 pint |
| 1 kg | 2 to 2¼ lb | 1 litre | 35 fl oz |

**Cover:** Peking duck (*recipe, page 42*) is probably the most famous dish to originate from the north of China and it is almost impossible to wander into a Chinese restaurant in the capital where it isn't served. The traditional way to enjoy Peking duck is wrapped in a light pancake with spring onion and hoisin sauce. A glass of rice wine or an ice cold Chinese beer, such as *Tsingtao*, is a perfect accompaniment.

**TIME-LIFE BOOKS**

COOKERY AROUND THE WORLD
English edition staff for *China: Peking and Shandong*
*Editorial Manager:* Christine Noble
*Editorial:* Felicity Jackson, Mark Stephenson, Kate Cann,
*Designer:* Dawn McGinn
*Production:* Justina Cox, Jenny Croxall

English translation by Isabel Varea for Ros Schwartz Translations, London

Published originally under the title *Küchen der Welt — Peking und Shandong* by Gräfe und Unzer Verlag GmbH, Munich

© 1995 Gräfe und Unzer Verlag GmbH, Munich

This edition published by Time-Life Books B.V. Amsterdam
Authorized English language edition
© 1996 Time-Life Books B.V.
First English language printing 1996

TIME-LIFE is a trademark of Time Warner Inc. U.S.A.

ISBN 0 7054 3540 7

Colour reproduction by Fotolito Longo, Bolzano, Italy
Output by Leaside Graphics, Luton, England
Printed and bound by Mondadori, Verona, Italy

**GRÄFE UND UNZER**

*Editor:* Dr Stephanie von Werz-Kovacs
*Editor-in-Chief:* Angela Hermann
*Designer:* Konstantin Kern
*Recipes tested by:* Traute Hatterscheid, Barbara Hagmann, Dorothea Henghuber, Christa Konrad-Seiter, Marianne Obermayr
*Production:* VerlagsService Neuberger & Shaumann GmbH, Heimstetten.
*Cartography:* Huber

**Thomas Gwinner** was born in 1960 and studied Classical and Modern Chinese and East Asian Art History. His interest in East Asian cuisine was built on during several years travelling in China, Taiwan, Hong Kong, Korea and Japan. For his Master's degree, he wrote a dissertation on tofu, while his doctoral thesis dealt with classical Chinese cookery literature. He also attended business school and is sales director for an international scientific publishing house.

**Zhenhuan Zhang** was born in 1951 in Shanghai where he learnt German and then taught at the School of Languages. He gained his doctorate at Heidelberg University and teaches Chinese at Mainz University. He not only collected famous recipes for this book, but also included favourite recipes supplied by his friends.

**Michael Brauner** is a graduate of the Berlin Fotoschule. He worked as an assistant to several French and German photographers and specialized in food photography for five years before setting up on his own in 1984. He now divides his time between his studios in Karlsruhe and Gordes in Provence.

**Zhenran Zhang** was born in 1957 in Shanghai. His work of over 20 years as a painter and calligrapher has been exhibited both in China and abroad.

**Picture Credits**

Illustrations: Zhenran Zhang

All photographs by Michael Brauner, Food Fotografie, except those listed below.

Cover: Graham Kirk, London. Pages 4-5: top left (turnip seller in Peking), Marianne Obermayr, Munich; top middle (children playing in the rain), Ina Schröter, Munich; top right (poster painter), Erhard Pansegrau, Berlin; middle (tourists in 19th century costume in the Forbidden City), bottom right (child and prayer bell at the Lamoist temple, Chengde) and bottom middle (master and pupil practice swordmanship), Martin Thomas, Aachen; bottom left (musicians by the Great Wall), Paul Spierenburg, Kiel. 8-9, 10: Erhard Pansegrau, Berlin. 11 (top): Paul Spierenburg, Kiel. 11 (bottom): Martin Thomas, Aachen. 12: Paul Spierenburg, Kiel. 13 (top): Ina Schröter, Munich. 13 (bottom): Martin Thomas, Aachen. 14: Paul Spierenburg, Kiel. 15 (top): Uli Franz/jd, Munich. 15 (bottom): Paul Spierenburg, Kiel. 16, 17: Uli Franz/jd, Munich. 18 (top): Ina Schröter, Munich. 18 (bottom): Uli Franz/jd, Munich. 19, 20: Martin Thomas, Aachen. 21: Paul Spierenburg, Kiel. 22 (top): Peter Fischer, Krefeld. 22 (bottom), 23: Martin Thomas, Aachen. 24: Uli Franz/jd, Munich. 25: Peter Fischer, Krefeld.

**Dedicated to Kwei Yin Yang**
in appreciation of your constant encouragement and valuable cooperation

**Special thanks to** the manager of the Shanghai Restaurant in Heidelberg, Mr Lao Kooi Cheng, and his *chef de cuisine*, Mr Chao Ping, for their support.